Enter If You Dare...

BOOK REVIEWS

Review:

With the release of their first book (*How to Haunt your House*) the Mitchell's established themselves as creators of the best book ever written on the subject. This book matches that....and perhaps even goes beyond. They just keep getting better. No review can do justice to the high quality of the writing and photos.

The book is full of great ideas on how to turn your house into the house kids (and adults) will remember all their lives. When they tell their children and grandchildren about trick or treating when they were a kid..."back in the day"...they will remember that one house...the house that really knew how to decorate for Halloween...the house that knew "How to Haunt". The one decorated using the Mitchell's books.

That is what this book will teach you. In plain step by step directions combined with the best high quality pictures and art work ever seen in a haunt book.

Lynne & Shawn Mitchell have firmly established themselves as the best in their field. Buying these books will be the first step on your road to creating "that house"...the one everyone will remember for decades.

These books raise haunting from a hobby to an art form!!!

Happy Haunting
PropMaster
www.halloweenpropmaster.com

Review:

Move over Martha, the real king and queen of Halloween have staged a cu de ta with their second book, *How to Haunt Your House 2*. I thought the Mitchell's would be hard pressed to top their first effort, but they have. This book is a must have for newbie haunters as well for experienced prop makers. It is visually stunning and worth the price just to have on your coffee table.

I spend an exorbitant amount of time looking at prop making tutorials and really appreciate how Lynne and Shawn break down the projects keeping things very simple. They cover all the basics from materials, hacking store bought props, fencing, gates, tombstones, animatronics to faux wood and stone. The projects in this book will keep you busy for years and help you to create an Award-Winning home haunt. Take your haunt or Halloween party to the next level and buy both volumes.

Chris Baker, G-Host
Hauntcast - Radio for Haunters and Halloween fanatics
www.hauntcast.net

Review:

The Home Haunters Association Team just finished reviewing the soon to be published second book titled *How to Haunt Your House*, by Shawn and Lynne Mitchell. Once again, this book has set the bar for "how to" haunt books. Once again, we would rate this book with our highest rating of five skulls?

The book covers a range of topics from basic craft technique through construction of complete props. In our opinion it is an extension of book one with more detail and more unique prop designs.

One of the beautiful features of these books is the clear writing styles and the illustration is out of this world. The clarity makes this book a treat for both the experienced and novice haunter. One example is the "foam technique section". In this section, the illustrations are so clear that you can see the every crack and crevice in the stone work. As haunters we all strive to reach new heights of realism in our designs.

This book truly brings that Theatrical/Hollywood effect to the props.

Another great example is the section on utilizing wiper motors for your haunt. Wiper motors are key for a lot of prop animation, but using them for the first time can bring challenges. This book de-mystifies their use in prop building.

All things considered, this book is the second masterpiece from Shawn and Lynne Mitchell. I am anticipating the publish date and adding this hardcopy to my collection. BRAVO!!!! We can't wait for book #3.

The Home Haunters Association Team
http://www.homehauntersassociation.com

Review:

The obscenely talented Mitchells have done it again. Volume Two of their popular house-haunting guide is just as good as its predecessor. So good, in fact, that it puts other haunted how-to books to shame.

This guide will teach you how to create both large and small-scale props using a combination of items from around your home and those readily available at most hardware stores. Their instructions are easy to follow and the photography is beautiful.

My favorite chapter shows how to transform cheap-looking store-bought items into impressively ghoulish props. Now I own many of the same inexpensive gargoyles, bats and busts that grace the book's pages, but none of mine look nearly as good as theirs. It's amazing what can be quickly and easily achieved with just a little paint when you know what you're doing. (And thanks to this book, now I do.)

"How To Haunt Your House - Book Two" is a must-have for any Halloween enthusiast.

HauntStyle.com

Review:

I have to say first and foremost, it was an absolute pleasure to review this book. I'm proud of the opportunity to critique a project that took so much time and precision. Again, we're dazzled with spooktacular lighting, stunning visuals and a simple to understand format. I was delighted with the step by step instructions. This book was packed with information and caused me as a reader to come up with multiple ideas for additional projects as I read the material. Basically, the book puts you in the mood. This book is a definite thumbs up. It's no doubt that Lynne and Shawn love what they do and enjoy sharing their happiness with others. 5/5 stars. I'm hoping to wind up with a *How To Haunt Your House* collection at some point.

Pete Henderson
www.hauntspace.com (founder)

Review:

In their first book, Lynne and Shawn Mitchell took you through a gorgeous and macabre world of Halloween prop-building to haunt your house. Book Two, I'm happy to say, is not a rehash of their first book, but a worthy companion that ambitiously expands on their haunting tutorials, while easily standing on its own with all new projects, styles and techniques, all presented in clear, glossy photos and instructions.

In their "dead"ication, the authors pay enthusiastic homage to all the things that go bump in the night. I can easily imagine being one their neighbors as summer begins to morph into autumn ... "Strange lights are often spotted in the late, night hours and the occasional, stray sounds of owls, hissing cats and long, drawn-out cries of wolves will be heard echoing down the driveway." This successfully sets the tone for the lush and gothic world we are about to enter, and the shadows cast by their props begin to look just a little bit too alive ... an effect we can produce by following their inspiring examples.

And what should we except from this book? Well, how about a full tutorial on building (and deconstructing for storage) an entire scale model gothic mausoleum, complete with an old, rusty wrought-iron gate? Hard to believe it's all achieved with wood frames, Styrofoam and PVC pipe! Stock your kitchen with apothecary jars full of strange, glowing liquids filled with creatures you can almost (but not quite) recognize. Construct huge gargoyle columns, fashion a complete crypt that doubles as a hide-away for your electronic components, create foggy, bubbling cauldrons and turn store-bought props and mannequins into ghoulish hags and decapitated brides.

If that's not enough, Lynne and Shawn devote a large section of their book on animated props. Using clear and detailed images, they show you the components you need, types of motors and connections, and suggested power supplies. Step-by-step, they take you through two motorized projects, one of a monster churning a pot by hand, and an undead creature turning its head in a cemetery. I would love to see videos of these completed projects on their website!

A book on building and designing props would certainly be fulfilling, but all of these projects are unified with chapters on how to present an enthralling entrance, inside decor (with tips on lighting and accessories), and images and layout tips for a fully-stocked cemetery.

I am astonished with their creativity, attention to detail, and willingness to peel back the moth-eaten curtains to teach you how everything is done. It's presented with lush, full-page images and eerie backgrounds to keep with the mood. This book proudly stands with their first volume, and I'll need to build an inspiring gothic bookcase to house them!

BOOK TWO

How To Haunt Your House

COPYRIGHT

Library of Congress Cataloging-in-publication Data
How To Haunt Your House, Book Two
/ Shawn and Lynne Mitchell

Library of Congress Control Number: 2009900509

ISBN 978-0-578-05054-6 (paperback)

DEADICATION

We love our fear of the unknown. We like mysterious, cold spots and things that make us jump. We smile at being caught off guard and laugh often when something makes our hair stand on end. We are at home with ghosts, and spooks, and creaky doors. It's Halloween again—*our favorite time of the year.* Time to embrace our fear of the dark and things that go bump in the night!

Neighbors will start to notice odd structures going up in our backyard in early August. Strange lights are often spotted in the late, night hours and the occasional, stray sounds of owls, hissing cats and long, drawn-out cries of wolves will be heard echoing down the driveway. By October, a permanent thick, gray fog will hover over our house as a multitude of fog machines are set in to place and tested. The Jack-o-lanterns will be lit and the skeletons hung. And endless yards of cobweb will be strung from every nook and cranny. The cauldron will be filled and candy will come out. The animated, black crow will call out, *"It' time! It's Halloween time again!"*

Suspense will build as this new Hallows' Eve approaches. There will be many to peak through our fence for a preview. We know they will tell their children that the sign has been posted by the roadside, inviting all once again to take a tour of, *The Mitchell Cemetery.* It is here, that spirits move around fallen stones of old and rise up from mounds of fresh-dug graves of earth ... visible to the, sometimes frightened eyes of passer-bys. Some won't make it past the open gate at the entrance. Others, won't want to leave... amazed at all the glowing tombstones and ghosts that walk around to greet them. Costumed hands of the smallest visitors will hold tight to mom and dad and an even tighter grip on plastic pails full of candy. It is our greatest joy to think, that these brave souls, will one day tell stories, about the house on *Penton Street...*

This book offers a glimpse of what once was... a memory of a Halloween's past and is dedicated to all those like us. We hope a chill runs up your spine, and your hair stands of end, and more than once, you will glance over your shoulder at the unknown sounds in the night. Listen. Listen carefully for that child-like voice inside to say, *"It's Halloween time again..."*

Lynne & Shawn

How To Haunt Your House
CONTENTS

Basic Tools & Materials You Can Use For Most Projects

Whether you're a hard core home haunter, a re-crafter of store bought items, or looking to create the most spooktacular party there ever was, there are a few handy tools to have on hand before you start.

1 Craft Paints
Black and white craft paints are essential. Other colors, such as red, brown, green and yellow could also be used.

2 Gauze or Cheesecloth
You'll find many uses for this versatile, light-weight material. It can be dyed, torn, painted and wrapped.

3 Drywall Compound
This is excellent for creating textures on all kinds of props and can be mixed with latex paint for a starting base color. Once dry, it can be painted further and made to resemble everything from marble to wood.

4 Wood Burning or Soldering Tool
These tools are perfect for sculpting detail into Styrofoam. Different woodburning tips can achieve a variety of effects. The heated tool melts Styrofoam quickly, but the results can be everything from chiseled stone to lettering. Use in a well ventilated area.

5 Craft Brushes
A variety of craft brush sizes are always handy for applying final details to props.

6 Serrated Knife
A serrated knife if useful for cutting Styrofoam. It creates a rough, uneven edge.

7 Craft Glue
Water-soluble craft glue or Gorilla glue will work for most projects and can be used on Styrofoam.

8 Toothpicks
Toothpicks are like straight pins for the home haunter. They are perfect for holding parts in place for a variety of projects in this book. Use the type that is pointed on both ends.

9 Hot Glue Gun & Glue Sticks
The hot glue gun is best tool in the home haunter's arsenal. Have several bags of glue sticks on hand to start with.

10 Heated Wire Cutter
Another tool for cutting and carving Styrofoam is the Wire Styrofoam Cutter. It creates smooth edges.

11 L Brackets
Any wood building projects that use the 1x2 wood will also use lots of L Brackets to join the two pieces of wood together at the corners.

12 PVC Pipe
Strong, yet light-weight, PVC is used in making interior, bone structures, fence poles and candle forms. Many sizes and thicknesses are available.

13 Duct Tape
An all around useful material in a variety of projects is duct tape. Use to shape a character's body or hold project pieces in place while you work.

14 Wood & Wood Screws
Excellent for building large prop structures or as interior skeletons of prop characters. Generally 1x2 wood is used. Heavier wood can also be used for extra stability.

15 Styrofoam
Styrofoam is found in hardware stores and is used as insulation in houses. Styrofoam comes in a variety of thicknesses, from half inch to 2 inches thick. There are two types of Styrofoam. White foam has a larger cell structure and comes in sheets of the largest thickness. Blue (or pink) foam has a tighter composition and is less messy than white foam when cut, but is available only in thinner sizes. Full sheet size is 4 feet by 8 feet. Styrofoam is great for creating large light-weight walls or several tomb-stones per sheet.

16 Wiper Motor, Wall Wart, or Pacemaker, Quick Connect, Power Supply Cord
If you want to animate your props these are some basic components you will need. *See page 72* for more details on motor projects.

17 Other Useful Items
Carbon paper, black and white spray paint, latex gloves, paver sand, zip ties, fabric dye, wire, wire cutters, PVC cutter, drill & drill bits, wax paper, Plexiglass, carpet glue, rope, pipe insulation, spray bottle, cardboard building form tube, Polymer Clay, Polymer clay mold forms, jewelry charms, beads or buttons, Styrofoam prop skulls and bones, faux fur, cages of various sizes and shapes, large and small sized jars, plastic cauldron, pond misters, Christmas tree lights, chicken wire, clothes hanger, old clothes or curtains

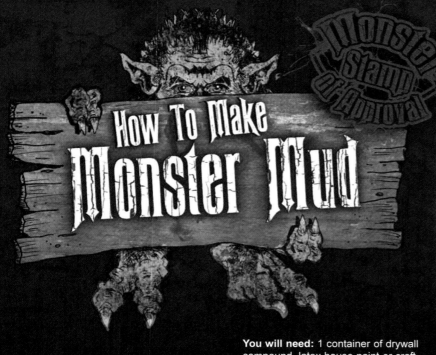

How To Make Monster Mud

Small Batch Mixing

You will need: 1 container of drywall compound, latex house paint or craft paints (any color/s), container for mixing, spoon, or drywall mixer attachment and drill to mix large batches (*optional*)

Monster-mud is a term first coined by Steve Hickman of *Terror Syndicate Productions*. However, the recipe and application have been used in the effects industry for some time. It is simple to make and can be applied to an unlimited list of craft projects that require some texture. It also works very well with Styrofoam. The *Monster Mud* creates a textured shell over the light-weight Styrofoam that can then be made to look like a variety of materials. Recycle some of that old paint sitting in the garage. It doesn't matter what colors you use or mix together. It will be used as a base for other colors on the Styrofoam "stone". How much compound needed depends on the project. Make a large batch in a bucket with a lid and you can store it for months. Mix roughly 5 parts drywall compound to 1 part paint and mix. A drywall mixer attached to a drill works best to mix large batches. A spoon and bowl will work for small batches. Use latex gloves and protect clothing and surfaces. *Monster Mud* will stain.

Drywall Compound

Latex Paint mixed with Drywall Compound for sand colored base

Mix any color craft paints for base color

Styrofoam Techniques
Part 2

How to Haunt Your House, Book One, showed you some basic Styrofoam uses. This chapter further elaborates on those techniques.

A ny kind of Styrofoam can be used for your prop creations. Blue or pink Styrofoam comes in thinner 4x8 foot sheets and can be found at most hardware stores. The cell structure of this Styrofoam is more densely packed and is less messy when cut. Packing Styrofoam pieces can also be recycled from shipping boxes. They come in all sizes, shapes, and thicknesses. These miscellaneous pieces can be glued, sculpted and attached as 3d parts, or as assembled architectural pieces on larger props. White 4x8 foot Styrofoam sheets come in sizes from ½ inch to 2 inches thick and have a larger cell structure. When cut, this crumbly texture can be used purposely to create rough stone edges or a worn prop appearance.

Large, flat pieces of Styrofoam can be cut with a straight edge and scoring. Once the piece is scored, hold one side of the score firmly against a flat surface, such as a table top, and with your other hand gently push down on the opposite scored side. The Styrofoam will snap apart with a clean, straight edge.

Styrofoam can be made to resemble just about anything. It's lightweight, inexpensive, and easy to work with. It can be used to make everything from small prop tombstones to larger, layered structures. Once the basic Styrofoam shape is cut, and the design drawn out with a permanent marker, heated tools are then used to shape, cut into, or sculpt the piece further. Do this in a well ventilated area and take precautions against fumes. As the heated tool is pressed into the Styrofoam, the Styrofoam quickly melts away from the hot edge. Practice on a sample piece first. You will need to work fast and this could take some practice before you get the hang of it.

Tools:

Various tools can be used to cut and shape Styrofoam. Shown on right are: battery operated hot wire cutter, wood burning tools with various tips, soldering iron, electric wire cutting tool, serrated knife, spray paint, and a heat gun with low setting. Spray paint and a heat gun can both be used to quickly roughen the edges of a Styrofoam prop.

Never leave heated tools unattended and use in a well ventilated area!

Shown Right: Spray paint on Styrofoam "eats" away at the material and a heat gun melts it. Both create a natural worn edge look. Use either method sparingly and in a well ventilated area.

Layered Carved Stone

Use the hot tool point on its side to create chiseled stone effect. Use craft or Gorilla glue to attach separate Styrofoam pieces. Push toothpicks all the way in to complete.

Wood Planks

Use the tip of a hot tool to draw wood grain lines in a plank size piece of Styrofoam. Roughen the edges for a worn look and quickly draw a few cut marks on the surface at random angles for scratches.

Lettering & Designs

Use a permanent marker to draw out your design. With a hot tool, held like a pencil, trace back over the design. Move the tool quickly or too much of the design could be melted away.

Cracks & Cut Marks

Hold the hot tool against the Styrofoam longer to melt out large cuts or holes. Melt away any sharp, or straight edges to create a worn away effect. For cut marks, start off pushing the tool a little harder into the Styrofoam, then gradually pull up until the tool no longer touches the surface. Do several of these parallel to each other for claw marks.

Crumbling Brick & Plaster

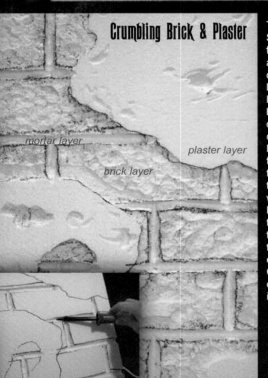

mortar layer

plaster layer

brick layer

Thicker pieces of Styrofoam work best for this effect. There are three levels of the design. The deepest level will be the mortar lines between the bricks. Don't go too deep, or the Styrofoam could break. The mid level is the brick surface. Use the hot tool to lower it just enough to leave a small edge where the plaster overlaps the brick. Roughen the brick surface with the side of the heated tool tip. The top, highest level, is the plaster. Create some random dent and scratch marks in the surface.

Natural Stone Wall

Draw out some random shape and size stones. Use the hot tool to lower the mortar between the stones. Further shape the stone edges for a rounder look.

Next Steps:

Once your Styrofoam prop has been completed, you can cover the surface with Monster Mud (*page 11*). When this is dry, it can be painted with craft paints.

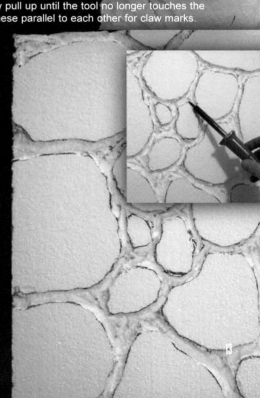

Making Your Own
Tombstone with Double Columns

Agatha & Christie
How They Died Is Still A Mystery...

You will need: 1 cutout 2 inch thick Styrofoam tombstone (4' x 4'), 1 cutout 2 inch thick Styrofoam book row (1' x 4'), carbon paper, enlarged template design or free hand drawn text template, ball point pen, black permanent marker, hot cutting tools of choice, serrated knife, Monster Mud (*page 11*), black, brown, white, craft paints (or colors of choice), paint brushes, sponge, cheesecloth or make-up wedge for applying paint, 2 garden statues (*see page 18*) or urns with faux flowers for columns, 1 cardboard building form tube cut in half, 2 Styrofoam tortilla containers (lid will not be used), 2 square cut pieces of Styrofoam (for column bases), 2 lengths of pool noodle sections or round pipe insulation (for ring at base of column), toothpicks, Gorilla Glue, latex gloves

TIP: Light large tombstones from the ground pointing up for an extra eerie look. A round, shop light with blue bulb was used here. Throw in a couple of creepy dolls and the look is complete. Visit, *www.howtohauntyourhouse.com* for information on making these dolls.

Large tombstones are a great focal point in the home haunt cemetery. This tombstone project is flanked by two columns, each topped with a faux painted statue. If statues aren't available, other props such as urns and faux flowers could be used. The columns could also be used on their own or used inside the haunted house.

3 Cover the entire column with ¼ inch thick *Monster Mud* or plain, drywall material. Leave overlapping steaks for texture around the column sides as shown. Be sure to cover the tortilla base cap with enough material to conceal the imprinted designs. Let dry.

4 If your column started off white, use black and white mixed craft paint to paint a gray base coat over the entire piece. If you used a pre-mixed Monster Mud recipe a base coat color may not be needed. Apply random shades from dark to light over the base coat. (Think about the surface of a multi-colored marble.)

Pool Noodle sections can be torn or cut apart and used.

Unpainted Statue
See pages 18-19 for Faux Metal paint FX

2 Place the form tube with pool noodle attached on the square-cut Styrofoam base. Trace position with permanent marker. Stand the toothpicks up in the base half an inch inside the traced pattern. Cover toothpicks with Gorilla Glue and slide into the pool noodle material. The Gorilla Glue and toothpicks will hold the pool noodle to Styrofoam base. Let dry.

5 Use a sponge or bunched up cheesecloth to gently dab at least two colors over the column surface. Some of the base colors should still show through. Here white and brown were used to create a pale marble color.

Styrofoam Tortilla Container Base with handles cut off.

Cardboard Building Form Tube

1 One section of Pool Noodle cut to fit. Attach noodle to form tube with Gorilla Glue and let dry.

6 Finally, using a paintbrush with a small tip (1/2 or smaller), drag the same colors (white and brown) in random diagonals, starting from the top and moving down. This will create the long streaks in the faux marble. Let dry.

Styrofoam Square Base

7 The Styrofoam Tombstone is created from two pieces, the curved back headstone and the row of books along the bottom. With a serrated knife, cut a piece of 2 inch thick Styrofoam sheet down to 4 foot x 4 foot. Cut another piece 1 foot x 4 foot for the book row. Cut a curved top on main piece similar to this one.

See pages 18-19 for Faux Metal paint FX on Statues

Agatha & Christie

How They Died Is Still A Mystery...

For an extra layer of detail, use a brush to add watered down, brown, craft paint drips. Let the paint run down the large cracks and column sides. This just adds another bit of wear and tear. Faux moss can also be applied as shown here. See *How To Haunt Your House, Book 1*, for more information on creating this effect.

8 Freehand various thicknesses of book spines on the 1'x4' piece of Styrofoam as shown.

9 Along the top edge, draw a curve for each book top. Use hot tools to create the details in the Styrofoam. If you have a round, flat tipped hot tool nib, this works well for pushing in the area along the top. Other nibs can also be used to press the Styrofoam down.

10 Hot tools melt Styrofoam quickly. Don't stay too long in any area. Always practice on a scrap piece of Styrofoam until you get the hang of it. Use a pointed hot tool to create the rest of the book details.

11 Use carbon paper and a ball point pen to trace out your tombstone text from a template or use permanent marker to free-hand a design. Use hot tools to push in the letters, cracks, and dents along the edge of the tombstone. Gorila Glue book row to the main tombstone. Let dry.

12 Cover the entire tombstone with Monster Mud (*see page 11*). Let dry. Use craft paints of black and white, applied loosely with a large paint brush or sponge, to further darken the base color. Let dry.

13 Using a small brush, apply black craft paint into all the letters, cracks and pushed-in details of the tombstone.

Next, apply similar colors, as used on the columns, with a sponge or cheesecloth. Let dry.

Paint details close-up

Painting Faux Metal

Ancient, weather-worn statues can add a layer of authenticity to the home haunt, both inside and out. The process uses only paint to transform everyday statuary into haunt-worthy accessories!

1 This statue was purchased at a home design center and was originally made for garden statuary. First, paint the entire piece with either metallic spray paint or brush-applied metallic craft paint. Let dry.

2 Using a sponge, make-up sponge, or bunched up cheesecloth, gently dab a mixture of dark green and black craft paint over the surface of the statue. Leave some of the metal paint showing through. Let dry.

Original Statue

You will need: black, white, dark and light green craft paints (or colors of choice), metallic spray paint or metallic brush-on paint of your choice, paint brushes, sponge, cheesecloth, or make-up wedge for applying paint, garden statuary prop

3 Mix some dark green and light green craft paint with a good amount of water. Use a paint brush to dab along the top of the stature (in this case, along the hairline works best) so that the paint runs down the statue. Do this until you have several paint runs all around the statue. Try not to disturb the wet paint trails too much. Let them dry completely before moving to the next step.

4 Sparingly, dab a medium or light green on the highest points of the statue. In this case, around the dress edge, the base, and the highest points of the hair. This adds a faux corrosive look to the metal.

Completed Statue

Applying Paint
You can use a variety of methods to apply paint: with cheesecloth, a paintbrush or with a sponge.

– with Cheesecloth

– with a Paintbrush

– or with Sponges

You will need: 2 inch and 3/4 inch Styrofoam, *Monster Mud (page 11)*, hot tool for sculpting, craft glue, craft paints, serrated knife, toothpicks, marker, paint brush, latex gloves

Tomb Cover
Hiding Your Electronics

F unction and design work together here as this tomb can cover a variety of tools needed in the home haunt arsenal. Whether its DVD players, sound speakers, plug outlets, or just extra bottles of fog juice, this hideaway is a quick and simple way to conceal what you don't want your audience to see. Keep in mind the amount of heat a piece of electrical equipment might give off and be sure to build it large enough for adequate air circulation and venting. This prop leaves one side completely open and has several open "cracks" for air to flow. The top also comes off for easy access.

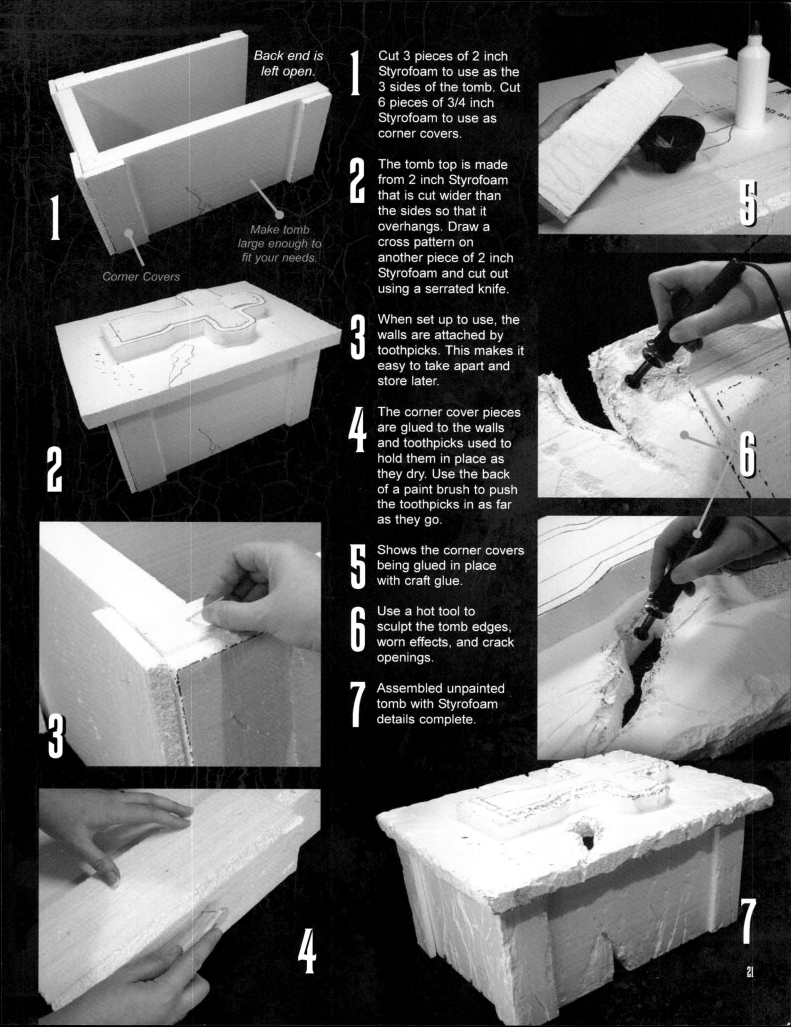

Back end is left open.

Make tomb large enough to fit your needs.

Corner Covers

1 Cut 3 pieces of 2 inch Styrofoam to use as the 3 sides of the tomb. Cut 6 pieces of 3/4 inch Styrofoam to use as corner covers.

2 The tomb top is made from 2 inch Styrofoam that is cut wider than the sides so that it overhangs. Draw a cross pattern on another piece of 2 inch Styrofoam and cut out using a serrated knife.

3 When set up to use, the walls are attached by toothpicks. This makes it easy to take apart and store later.

4 The corner cover pieces are glued to the walls and toothpicks used to hold them in place as they dry. Use the back of a paint brush to push the toothpicks in as far as they go.

5 Shows the corner covers being glued in place with craft glue.

6 Use a hot tool to sculpt the tomb edges, worn effects, and crack openings.

7 Assembled unpainted tomb with Styrofoam details complete.

8

Tomb Cover
Hiding Your Electronics

9

Covering the Styrofoam with Monster Mud.

8 Add a layer of *Monster Mud (see page 11)*. Wear latex gloves to spread it around. Be sure to get *Monster Mud* in all the details. Use a brush if necessary (*see photos A & B*). Let dry.

9 Mix some black and white craft paint together to get a gray color. Paint the tomb (*see photo C*). Let dry. Paint all the carved in areas with black, craft paint with a small paint brush.

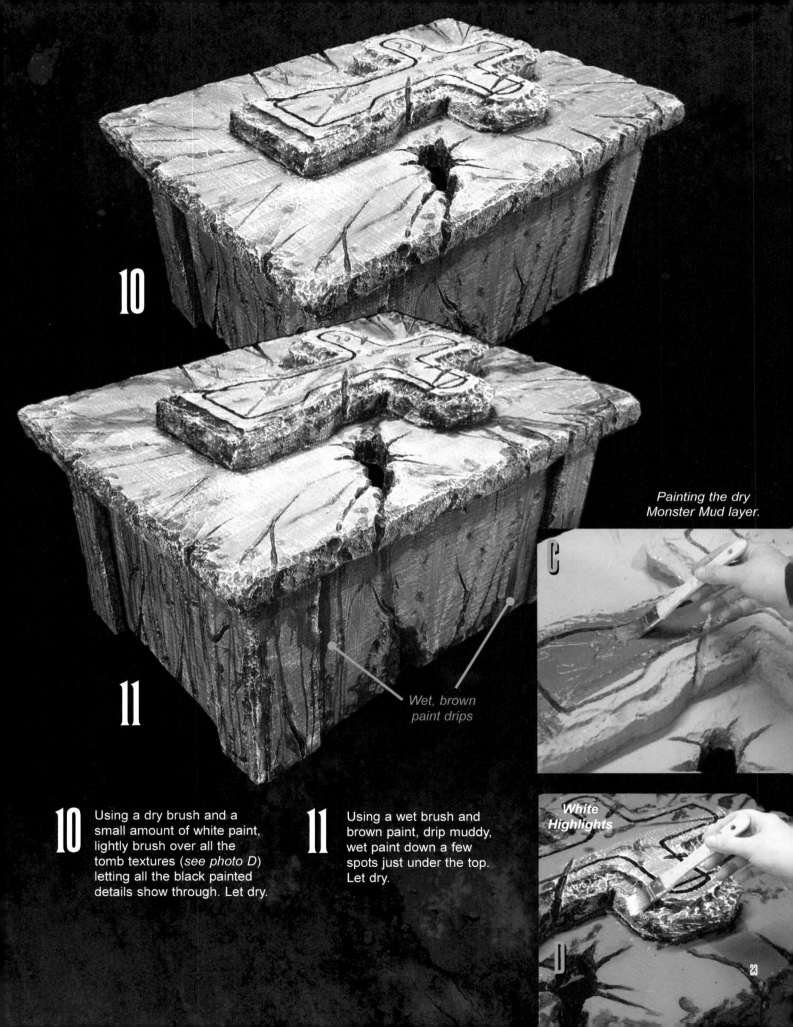

10

11

Painting the dry Monster Mud layer.

C

Wet, brown paint drips

10 Using a dry brush and a small amount of white paint, lightly brush over all the tomb textures (*see photo D*) letting all the black painted details show through. Let dry.

11 Using a wet brush and brown paint, drip muddy, wet paint down a few spots just under the top. Let dry.

White Highlights

D

Bride's Tomb
Creating A Large Scale Prop

You will need: 1x2 wood, "L" brackets, wood screws, 2 inch thick Styrofoam, 3/4 inch Styrofoam, Monster Mud, craft paints, fabric strips, toothpicks, paintbrush, serrated knife, 2 hinges, ½ inch PVC poles cut to size, PVC cutter, drill with 7/8 drill bit, duct tape, hot glue gun, glue sticks

T he best thing about large scale props in your home haunt setting is their usefulness. You can put things in them, hide things behind them or cover up parts you don't want to be seen. They also help fill out a setting quickly and make it seem more realistic by having a variety of structures sizes. One of the most important things to keep in mind is how it will be disassembled and stored once the event is over. It's unlikely family members will want to look at a mausoleum all year long in the back yard and the family dog may get a complex if forced to live in this new dog house…so a little planning a head can go a long way. You will want some type of framework and a way to attach and remove the Styrofoam walls easily.

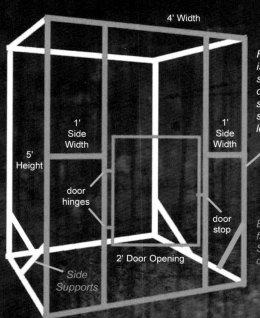

4' Width

Front wall and door is one complete section. When disassembling the structure, this section can be left intact.

5' Height

1' Side Width

1' Side Width

door hinges

door stop

Build wooden frame first, the add Styrofoam pieces cut to fit structure.

2' Door Opening

Side Supports

A front stone step, inscribed with the word "Beloved" is placed on top of some skulls.

1 First determine the approximate size the structure will be. Sheets of Styrofoam are 4 foot by 8 foot. Keeping the depth of your structure 4 foot or less and, no more than, 8 foot high would make things easier. Create a front wall and door section as shown above. Add a simple box frame to this section using L brackets and wood screws. Use two more lengths of wood to create a door opening at the front. Screw side support pieces at an angle to keep the structure from shifting.

2 **Door Assembly:** The door should fit inside the front opening with some space free on both sides, to allow for it to open. Space out a number of places to drill 7/8 inch holes along the top and bottom of the door frame. Cut slightly different lengths of ½ inch PVC pole to create bars. Hot glue in place. Spray paint entire door black. Let dry. Attach door frame to one side of mausoleum front with 2 hinges. A piece of scrap wood was added the opposite side, as a door stop, to keep the door from swinging in.

Inside the mausoleum is a painted box that has been topped with a piece of Styrofoam for a small crypt.

3 Create Styrofoam parts (*see pages 26-27 for construction*) and use fabric ties to attach the Styrofoam to the wooden structure.

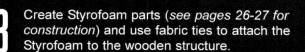

4 If using a crypt inside, place a box in center of the room. Cover with a piece of Styrofoam for a crypt top. Create a second piece to cover the box front. For a more detailed crypt, *see page 20*.

Styrofoam walls and ceiling attached with fabric ties.

5 Detail all the walls with a hot tool using the same methods described on *pages 12-13*. Create cracks, scratches, dents or wording to complete the look of your structure.

Front wall and door is one complete section. When disassembling the structure, this section can be left intact.

6 Once all the pieces have been *Monster Mudded* and are dry, paint the whole structure with craft paints using the same method as on the tombstones (*see page 14-15*).

Constructing the Styrofoam Parts

Each of the three bride's tomb walls have a separate base. The **base** is made from 2 inch thick Styrofoam. On each end, insert a 24 inch **fabric strap** in two cut double slits, which will be used to tie the piece to the wooden structure. Before cutting the slits, cover the spot with a piece of duct tape on both the front and back of the Styrofoam. This will help to reinforce the area when the fabric strap is inserted.

On top of the base will sit the wall. The **wall** is made using 3/4 inch Styrofoam. On top of this piece, is added two side **Edge Covers** of 3/4 inch Styrofoam. Create several 2 inch and 3/4 inch thick Styrofoam bricks in random places. At each corner, insert a fabric strap using the method described. Leave the ends loose on the back of the wall. Attach all wall pieces using toothpicks and craft glue. Let dry. Note, that the back wall of the structure can be left plain if it will not be visible.

Create two, smaller, **side walls for the front** of the structure. These will fit on either side of the door. Be sure to leave enough space for the door to open. Start with a layer of 3/4 inch Styrofoam to form a shallow "L" shape for the right side panel. Mirror this for the left side panel. Create a 2 inch thick Styrofoam base using the same height as the side walls. Glue this base piece to the 3/4 inch layer. Create two side strips of 3/4 inch Styrofoam and glue down also. Create the fabric strip openings near each corner and insert the fabric for each.

Over the two, front side walls will be a simple, length of Styrofoam as a **cap**. It is attached horizontally over the side, front panels using toothpicks. This makes it easy to remove.

The **roof** is a piece a four foot width of Styrofoam that is longer than the structure. It should overhang the front by around six inches. Where the piece rests on the wooden structure, place a fabric strip for each of the corners. This will tie the roof to the wooden frame.

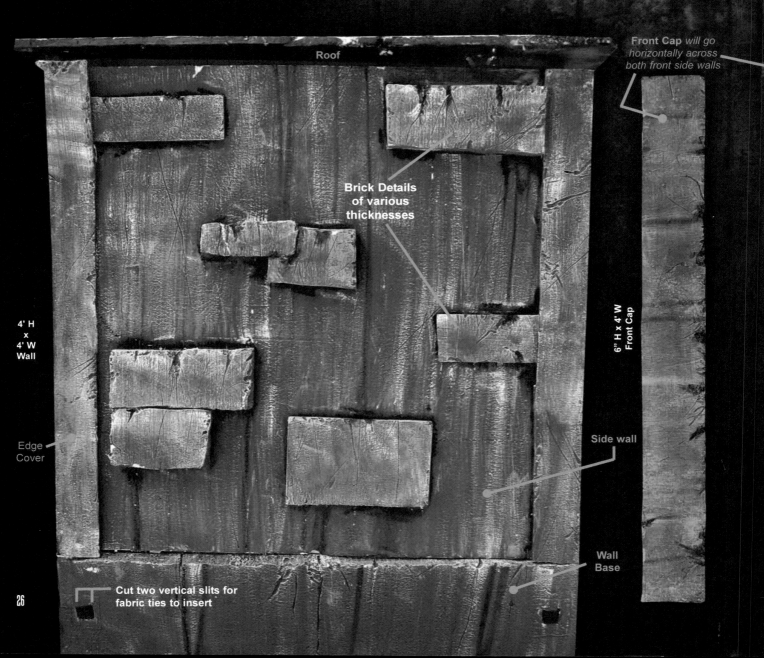

Roof

Front Cap will go horizontally across both front side walls

Brick Details of various thicknesses

4' H x 4' W Wall

6" H x 4' W Front Cap

Edge Cover

Side wall

Wall Base

Cut two vertical slits for fabric ties to insert

Fabric Ties

Fabric Ties are used to hold the Styrofoam to the wooden structure. Cover the Styrofoam area with duct tape, front and back, and make two cuts with a serrated knife for a fabric strip to pass through. Paint over any tie parts that show on the outside.

Back

Front

Unassembled Styrofoam Parts

Front Cap

Roof

Left Wall & Base Board

Step

Back Wall & Base Board

Front Side pieces

Crypt Wall Face

Crypt Top Cover

Right Wall & Base Board

Step and Crypt pieces are optional. See page 25 for more photos.

Door Hinges

Door PVC Bars

1' Side Panel Width

1' Side Panel Width

Insert Fabric Ties in Styrofoam anywhere close to a wooden support area. They will all tie on the inside of the structure.

Side Supports

Wall Base attached before adding side wall

Left and Right Front Side Walls

1'4" Side Panel Base Width

1'4" Side Panel Base Width

Spooky Chandelier

Achieving a thick, realistic spider's web can be done using hot glue sticks, a web shooter and an air compressor. It takes only a few minutes to spray the fine webs of hot glue and cover a chandelier using this method. Add some flicker-flame bulbs, some plastic spiders and you have the perfect haunted house accessory!

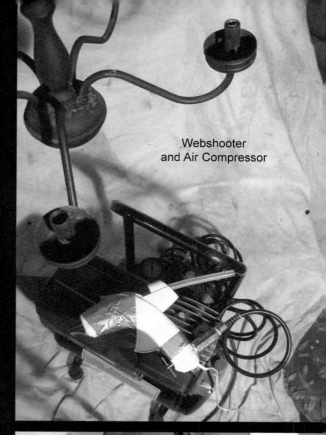

Webshooter and Air Compressor

1 The hot glue gun web shooter is a re-engineered hot glue gun and can be purchased online from many Halloween shops or can be built by following online tutorials. Once you have all these items, clear out the kids and the pets and hang the chandelier in a secure spot with a tarp underneath. Cover any areas you don't want hot glued. You will be spraying HOT glue, so take any necessary precautions.

2 Follow all instructions provided for using the air compressor and webshooter. Once the air compressor is ready and the glue gun web shooter is attached, plugged in and heated up, you can begin shooting the web. Carefully rotate the suspended chandelier so that all sides are covered. Continue webbing until desired layer thickness is achieved.

3 Last, add a length of black plastic chain to suspend the fixture and add flicker bulbs to the sockets. Wrap the chandelier electrical cord in or around the chain. Attach to the ceiling with hook. Gently add in a few plastic spiders into the webs for a final spooky touch.

Tip: Hang more than one spooky chandelier in a room and at different heights to add more drama.

You will need: 1 chandelier rewired to be used as a plug in fixture, air compressor, hot glue gun web shooter, 1 or more bags of glue sticks, length of black plastic chain, flicker bulbs, ceiling hook, plastic spiders (*optional*), and tarp

The Witches' Pantry

1 Create your own label or download this label from our website. Cut out label leaving some of the white paper around the edge.

2 Use rubber cement to attach label to glass bottle. Add glow-in-the-dark paint and water for the liquid inside. See *pages 32-33* for more ideas on creating bottle contents.

3 Press the label firmly to the bottle. Apply more rubber cement if needed. Wrinkles are ok. The label is meant to look old and worn.

4 Use either a golden-brown or a black permanent marker to color in the white outer border of the label. You want the ink to bleed through to the back side of the label edge.

Download any of the labels shown from our website: www.howtohauntyourhouse.com

When going through the haunted house, one might stumble upon the witches' pantry. Strange bottles of potions with sinister looking ingredients are tucked into shady corners and cabinets. Imaginative labels with descriptive words like *potion, brew, extract* or *distilled* cover the dusty bottles. What possible cures or curses might these concoctions contain?

The final bottle glows under blacklight.

5 Carefully roll up the label edges all the way around using your fingernail.

6 Add any details to the bottle that will go with the label theme, such as, ribbons or jewelry charms. See *pages 32-33* for more ideas.

7 Use either hot glue or melted wax to further seal the bottle. Be sure to always keep these breakable bottles away from small children's reach!

Custom Bottle Materials

These are just a few of the materials that could be used to create the witches' pantry bottles: a hot glue gun, glue sticks, scissors, bottles in various sizes and shapes, craft paints, glow-in-the-dark paints, jewelry charms, scrapbook charms, beads, permanent markers (various colors), string, jute, ribbon, plastic spiders, insects or snakes, rubber cement, color waxes, stained glass liquid leading, food coloring.

Polymer Clay is used for making the cork toppers. It can be found under several brand names in most craft stores. Once sculpted or pressed into molds, it is baked in the oven at a low temperature or air dried, according to instructions, and later painted. Always follow the manufacturer's instructions for using Polymer Clay.

Making Custom Witches' Bottles

Vintage Vampire Blood

Under blacklight

Distilled Spider Venom

Mix glow-in-the-dark white paint with water for the milky liquid contents. Add one black, rubber spider to the liquid. Attach label using rubber cement. Tint the edges of label with a gold-brown permanent marker and roll up the label edges using fingernail. Use the same marker to tint the glass along the top, bottom and sides. To do this, color in small sections at a time on the glass with the marker then quickly rub with a cloth to remove any harsh marker lines. Wrap black thread around cork to attach the small, black, spider jewelry charm. Use hot glue around the cork and bottle opening to seal.

Mix red food coloring with water for bottle contents. Attach aged label with rubber cement. Tint label edges with a gold-brown permanent marker and roll up label edges using your fingernail. Wrap a black ribbon around the bottle neck and hot glue a red, faux jewel and a black, rose jewelry charm at the end of ribbon. The bottle top is sealed by dripping black wax over the cork.

Laughing Spirits

This bottle is filled with yellow food coloring tinted water and beads. The cork topper is hand sculpted using Polymer Clay to form a small creature who is sticking out his tongue and wearing a wizard's hat. Once the Polymer Clay has hardened (*per clay instructions*), paint using craft paints of brown and gold. To make your own sculpted figure, start off using a press mold to form the face and hands. From here, roll up more clay to form arms and a body. Begin shaping all together to create something new. Use hot glue to attach creature to cork and to seal cork to bottle. The label design is attached using rubber cement. The label edges are tinted using a gold-brown permanent marker. Roll the label edges up using your fingernail.

Ectoplasm Extract

Create the ectoplasm strands by holding a hot glue gun high above a plate filled with water and letting the hot glue fall into the water in random circles. Continue until you have enough to loosely fill the bottle. Attach the aged label to the bottle and color the label edges with gold-brown permanent marker. Roll up the label edges using fingernail. Wrap bottle neck with a ribbon and attach a jewelry charm. Drip black wax over cork to seal. The Ectoplasm, hot glue strands will glow under blacklight.

Wolf's Bane

Fill bottle with dried Oregano leaves. Affix label to bottle using rubber cement and curl up edges with fingernail. The bottle topper is made using Polymer Clay. After the clay has hardened, it can be painted using brown craft paints and highlighted with a metallic paint for a bronze sculpture effect. A small metal charm is attached with hot glue.

There are many books available on working with Polymer Clay should you want to learn more.

Red Devil Potion

Add red food coloring to water for liquid. Seal around cork with hot glue. The bottle topper is made using Polymer Clay. When clay has hardened, the figure is painted with black, craft paint. Once dry, paint red highlights over the figure to make the details stand out. Attach figure to cork with hot glue. Drip black wax around bottle neck for added detail. Attach label with rubber cement. Color in label edge with a permanent, black marker and roll up label edge with fingernail for an aged look.

Good Luck Potion & Charms

This potion bottle is filled with green food coloring and water. Bottle topper is created using Polymer Clay and hardened according to manufacturer's instructions. Paint figure with gold paint. Let dry. Rub dark glaze or paint into surface details then wipe away to leave dark color only in the lower details of the figure. Wrap figure neck with gold ribbon and attach good luck charms. Label is attached with rubber cement. Tint label edges with gold-brown, permanent marker and roll up label edges using fingernail.

Green Thumb Elixir

Fill elixir bottle with 3 drops of green, food coloring and water. Seal bottle opening and cork with hot glue. Drip green wax over cork sides and hot glue two small, faux leaves and a colorful bead with plant designs on top of cork. Attach bottle label with rubber cement. Tint label edges with green, permanent marker and roll up label edges with fingernail.

Prophesy Potion

Fill bottle with a few drops of food coloring (any color) and water. Seal cork in place with hot glue. Attach label with rubber cement. Tint label edges with black, permanent marker. Roll up label edges with fingernail. Starting at the top of the bottle, create swirly lines of hot glue. Cover cork with more hot glue so that it resembles melted wax. On the top, place an interesting button or bead. Once the hot glue is cool, dry brush all of the hot glue with gold paint. Let dry.

Mummy Dust

Wrap thin strand of tea dyed gauze around bottle as shown. Hot glue ends in back. Attach a small loop of Egyptian-colored beads near the bottle opening. Attach label with rubber cement. Tint label edge with gold-brown, permanent marker and roll up label edges with fingernail. Fill bottle with coco powder. Seal cork with hot glue.

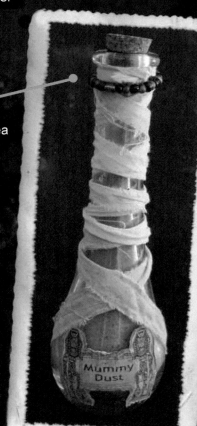

Haunt Tips

Place bottles in groups or in rows with a battery operated light or blacklight behind. This will light up the strange contents for an even more dramatic effect.

Dust the bottles with a makeup brush and foundation powder for a aged look (like an old bottle from the cellar). Overlay with cheesecloth spider webs.

Use small, doll heads in place of Polymer clay sculptures.

Spider's Web Bottle

To create the spider's web along the outside of the bottle, you will need to create some liquid, stained glass leading lines (found in craft stores). Squeeze out several five inch long, straight, leading lines on a piece of glass or mirror. Let dry completely. Use an Xacto knife to carefully remove one line at a time and apply to bottle. The faux leading will naturally stick to the glass. Create all the vertical webs first. On the horizontal webs, create a downward curve between each vertical web. Use hot glue to hold ends of leading in place. Add four drops of black food coloring mixed with water. Seal cork with wax or hot glue. Finally, attach a skull and cross bone jewelry charm.

Wise Woman Blend

Fill a tall bottle with a mix of old herbs. Bottle topper face and hand is made using press mold and Polymer Clay. Another flat piece of Polymer clay is wrapped around for the cloak. Harden clay, according to manufacturer's instructions. Paint figure with dark brown paint. Let dry. Brush small amount of green craft paint on highest parts of figure for a patina finish. Hot glue figure to cork and seal cork with more hot glue. Once cool, paint the hot glue green. Let dry. Wrap the bottle neck with jute, knot and leave the ends frayed. Attach a small jewelry charm with hot glue. Attach bottle label with rubber cement. Color label edges with gold-brown, permanent marker. Roll up label edges with fingernail for aged look.

Wise Woman Blend

Goblins' Teeth

Use Polymer Clay to hand form the goblins' teeth in a variety of sizes and shapes. Tint the teeth with brown and yellow craft paint. Fill the bottle with the teeth. Using more Polymer Clay, a tall hat shaped goblin was created and tied with a Polymer rope. Harden clay as directed. Paint the figure in light brown craft paint. Paint the rope gold. Let dry. Lightly brush the raised areas of the figure with black paint. Attach the figure to the cork with hot glue. Cut a small piece of tea dyed cheesecloth and place over the bottle opening. Press in the cork and seal with hot glue.

Hacked! Bride

Store-bought Props Redone

Not only has this bride-to-be lost her head, but she has lost her mind if she thinks she is scary enough for the home haunt! Originally a store-bought prop, this headless bride was given a complete make-over. Now when this animated prop opens her eyes and calls out mournfully to her audience she will be worthy of the title, *The Headless Bride*.

You will need: Torn cheesecloth, or any old, frayed cloth, white wig, prop bones or rib cage parts, neck bone, red yarn, blue, white, brown, black, and red craft paints, sponge or make-up sponge, paintbrush, small piece of tubing, hot glue gun, glue-sticks.

Head Hack

Plain, wig was removed. Face was painted with blue, black, red and white craft paints. Very large black circles were painted around the eyes. Lips were painted red. The cheekbones and neck were accented with black and highlighted with blue. Around the neck base was painted red. A piece of rubber tubing was hot glued to the bottom of the neck. Several strands of red yarn were also hot glued around the tubing.

Before

Before

TIP: Most white objects or fabric will glow when exposed to Blacklight. White that has been *grunged* up first will have a much creepier effect.

Body Hack

Glue a small piece of spine bone (usually found in a bag of bones prop) to the top of the neck stump. The neck and hands are painted light blue. The dress has been torn open on one side of the chest. More prop bones were hot glued inside the exposed area. Tear several lengths of white cheesecloth and tie around the wrists. Drape some more cheesecloth strands around neck to hang down the front of the dress. Use brown and black craft paints around dress edge and in a few random places as shown. Drip some red paint around the neck and chest.

After

Hot glue piece of tubing or neck bone as neck piece. Glue red yarn strands to complete the look.

After

Hacked! Hag

You will need: an old dress with long sleeves, dyed and torn cheese-cloth, or any old, frayed cloth, 1 long gray wig, necklace of prop bones, fingers or other body pieces, distressed witch's hat, brown, black, green and yellow craft paints, spray varnish, sponge or make-up sponge, paintbrush, hot glue gun, glue-sticks.

Store-bought Props Redone

What self-respecting hag would be caught dead in this *before* outfit? Too much glitter-sparkle and not enough swamp-grunge! A few odds and ends, some Halloween accessories, an old dress and a new hairdo will turn this out-of-the-box fashion disaster into a haunt-couture statement.

1 Remove the character's hat and hair. Using craft paints and a sponge, apply a dark, base coat color to the entire face, neck and hands. In this case, we used brown, but any color will work. Be sure to fill in all the crevices. Do not paint the eyes or the Velcro for attaching the hair. Let dry. Next, lightly sponge a lighter color over these same parts, leaving any low areas and crevices alone. The base color should show through from these low areas. Let dry. Add any other colors for skin highlighting, such as greens and yellows. Use a sponge or brush to apply. Add some black around the eyes and inside the ears, as shown. Let dry. Spray varnish the painted areas for protection. Let dry.

2 The character's original dress can be removed or left on and a new (old) dress added on top of the original dress. If the dress is too long, it can be cut or torn along the bottom edge to shorten it.

3 Attach old, cloth remnants or dyed, torn cheesecloth to any parts that need some extra coverage or to add to the old hag look. Tie a cloth belt around the figure's middle.

4 Now, accessorize with any beads, props or appropriate items for your character's look.

5 Hot glue or Velcro the long, gray haired wig to the head. Rub various handfuls of wig hair between your hands to create tangles. Twigs and leaves can also be added into the hair with small dab of hot glue. Add new distressed hat.

6 If the character is an animated prop, test to make sure the moving parts can still move freely.

Before

After

Now all those detailed wrinkles stand out!

The Gatekeeper

Guardian to the entrance of the outdoor or indoor home haunt setting, this imposing sentinel is sure to have all eyes casting a wary glance as visitors pass by. He holds the book of names, checking those who pass through, to see if they are among the living…or the *dead*.

You will need: a large bucket, 2 lengths of 1x2 wood, wood screws, two 1 inch diameter PVC poles, pipe insulation tubing, several yards of fabric or a purchased monk robe, *Monster Mud (page 11)*, Needle and thread (*or sewing machine*), strong gauge wire or wire coat hangers, prop skull, plastic chain, duck tape, black and white spray paint, plastic grocery bags, book prop (*page 42*), 2 inch thick Styrofoam, 3/4 thick Styrofoam, string, drill with ¼ inch drill bit, prop hands (*optional*)

A blue spot light was used here at ground level and pointed up at the prop.

Add some moss and cheesecloth spider webbing for final extra details.

1 The skeleton body is supported by a 1x2 wooden "spine" that also forms a ground stake. Place this stake into a weighted down bucket to keep it steady. Use a piece of this same wood to create a hip and shoulder cross section. Add another cross part at the foot area. Screw these to the spine wood.

Screw in several wood screws, half way in only, along the back of the spine to the hips. Also add one on each end of the shoulder wood and one on each end of the hip wood. These will be used to attach wires.

For the rib cage area, form a basic rib cage shape using wires. Wrap the wire around wood screws and spine wood to hold in place. Cut PVC pipe into 2 arm length sections for each arm and 2 leg sections for each leg. Drill ¼ hole on both ends of each PVC section. Use more wire to connect each arm section together and each leg section together leaving gap in between. Stuff joint gap with a ball of plastic bags. Wrap loosely with duck tape. Knee should be able to bend and be posed for later.

Connect prop hands or hands made of wire, as shown below, to the wrist PVC holes. Connect each arm and leg to the wood frame using wire and the wood screws. Screw head to neck or slip over pole end if the head is hollow. Now that all the parts are added, use pipe installation tubing, or plastic bags, to add bulk to the wires and PVC limbs. Tape in place.

Using more wire bend the arms at the elbows and pose the legs. Prop end of one leg up on the wood foot support so that the leg appears to be bent at the knee. Wrap with wire and tape to keep in position.

1

Wood

Parts wrapped and taped for added bulk.

Wood

Knee Joint

Wood

2

The skeleton structure does not have to exactly match this one. It just needs to resemble a skeleton body shape and be able to hold up the Monster Mud clothing.

One method to create hands is simply taping together five wires for fingers. Cover each finger fabric or plastic and tape in place. Cover this layer with duct tape, *Monster Mud* and paint as needed.

2 The Gatekeeper is draped in fabric covered with *Monster Mud*. If you do not have a monk's robe, sew two wide lengths of fabric into two tubes with both ends open for the sleeves. Set aside. For the main gown, sew up the sides of two lengths of fabric. Leave open the arm areas. The opening should fit the arm piece already assembled. Sew across the shoulder tops, leaving the head area open.

Sew the arms to the arm openings. Dip the fabric or costume into a bucket of prepared *Monster Mud* and thoroughly coat. Remove as much excess mud as possible from the cloth. Slip onto the figure skeleton form.

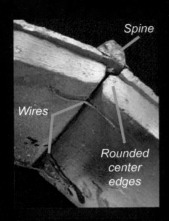

Spine

Wires

Rounded center edges

Cut Styrofoam book page edges at an angle

Creating The Book

Use two pieces of 2 inch (*book pages*) and 3/4 inch thick (*book covers*) Styrofoam. Use a hot wire tool or serrated knife to cut 2 inch thick Styrofoam with angled outer edges to resemble over-sized book page blocks. Use same tool to round the center edges (*center book fold*).Cut another 2 inch thick "spine" with rounded outer edges. Arrange parts to look like an open book, slightly angled, not flat (*as figure on right holds it*). Tape the spine to the 3/4 inch thick covers. Glue the pages to the covers. Run two wires through whole book to hold together and in position. Twist wires at spine. *Monster Mud* the whole book. Let dry. Paint same as the Gatekeeper.

3 Add another piece of *Monster Mud* coated fabric over the head and shoulders. Arrange the folds for dramatic effect. When it is dry it will have the appearance of having been sculpted out of stone. Dip the plastic chain in *Monster Mud* and wrap around the body as desired. Wire together the ends. Place the book prop into the arms and adjust the hands around it. Wire into place if needed. Let dry.

4 Once *Monster Mud* is dry, use a marbleizing paint technique using black and white spray paint over the whole figure and book. First, spray black randomly over figure, especially in crevices and under hood. Next, lightly spray white over the highest parts of figure. Once dry, use a very wet brush to throw white and black paint splatters over figure for a speckled stone appearance. Let dry.

The final painted Gatekeeper and Book of Names

5 Finally, remove the bucket and secure the figure in the haunt area so that it will not fall over. More wire can be added to attach him to a post or structure. Add dramatic lighting, more moss, spider webs or anything else to complete the look of the Gatekeeper.

Use moss and cheesecloth spider webbing to conceal wires.

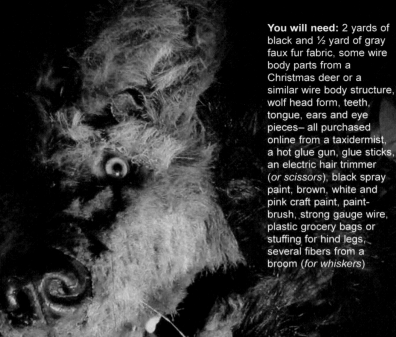

You will need: 2 yards of black and ½ yard of gray faux fur fabric, some wire body parts from a Christmas deer or a similar wire body structure, wolf head form, teeth, tongue, ears and eye pieces– all purchased online from a taxidermist, a hot glue gun, glue sticks, an electric hair trimmer (*or scissors*), black spray paint, brown, white and pink craft paint, paintbrush, strong gauge wire, plastic grocery bags or stuffing for hind legs, several fibers from a broom (*for whiskers*)

1

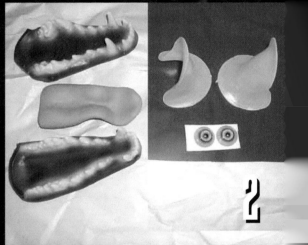

2

3

Wolfenstien
Creating A Wolf Prop

reate your own Wolfenstien from bits and pieces around the re-crafter's lab. It won't take 10,000 volts of electricity to scare up this creation, but place this menacing beast in your haunt scene and it will be ure to add some hair raising howls!

1 Upper and lower jaw and neck of a wolf form purchased from a taxidermist.

2 Teeth sections, tongue, ears forms and eyes also purchased from a taxidermist.

3 An electric hair trimmer is used to trim

Spray paint the purchased upper and lower jaw pieces black. Let dry. Assemble the teeth and tongue. Hold a piece of gray faux fur to the upper head piece and measure out to the back of the head. Cut. Use the electric trimmer to shorten the fabric hairs for the face area. Leave longer fur towards the neck area. Gluing a small bit at a time, hot glue the fabric down starting just behind and around the nose. Smooth out fabric after gluing. Cut holes for eyes to be placed in. Cut whisker lengths of the broom strands and hot glue to sides of snout. Attach the eyes.

White craft paint is lightly applied with a brush to highlight the fur for eye brows and sides of upper snout. A small amount of brown and pink is dry brushed onto the tip of the nose to blend in with the faux fur.

Shows upper jaw from underneath.

Side view

Spray painted lower jaw before fur is added.

Faux fur being applied to top of head.

Glue another piece of trimmed gray fabric to the lower jaw bottom. Cover the inside of the ears with untrimmed gray fur and the outside with untrimmed black fur. Hot glue both in place. Once the black body fur is added it will overlap the gray head fur as shown in the completed photo.

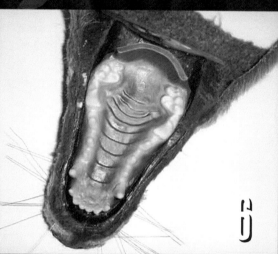

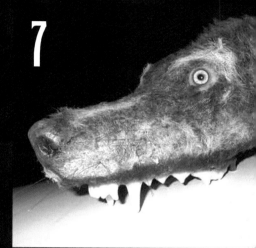

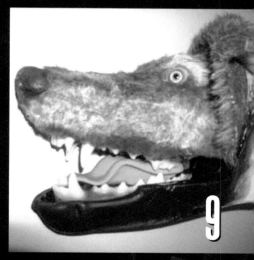

Completed wolf head

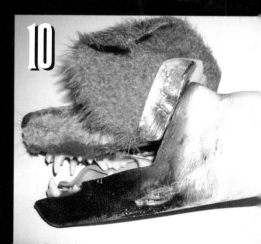

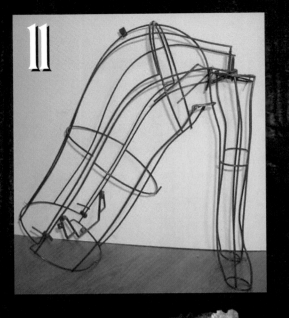

11 A wire form from a Christmas reindeer is used for the body here. You could also make a similar shape using wire or coat hangers.

12 Cover the legs with the untrimmed black faux fur. Hot glue into place. Attach the head to the body using wire and hot glue.

13 The back is covered in more untrimmed black fur. The hind legs are curved pieces of fabric that have been stuffed and attached at the sides of the body with hot glue. Create two hind feet the same way. Wolf should look as if he is sitting with his hind legs on the ground.

Stuffed hind legs and feet

14 The back of the wolf head is raised up with plastic bag stuffed under the fur. Cut a long piece of black faux fur to a point and glue down between the ears and toward the nose as shown below to complete your Wolfenstien.

Haunt Tips

Once Wolfenstien is placed in the haunt setting, set up a tape recorder with wolf howls and growls next to him.

Hang a motion activated light to trigger when someone comes near this prop to reveal him unexpectedly!

14

Extra piece of pointed long faux fur is added to forehead.

Creature Cages

You will need: Cages of various size, color, and shape, any sort of store-bought or handmade creatures to put in the cages. Moss, straw, torn paper, pine straw, or leaves can be added for cage bedding. *Optionally*, add faux bones, body parts or creature remains to the cages.

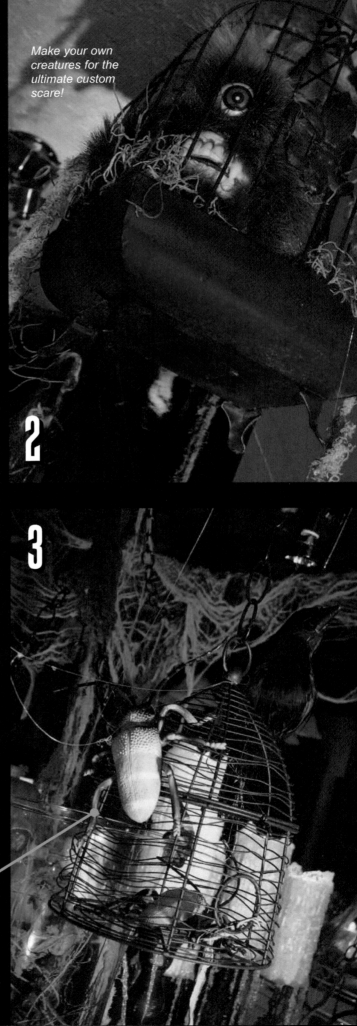

Make your own creatures for the ultimate custom scare!

2

3

1

H anging from rafters, doorways, or dark corners of a room, cages filled with all manner of creatures make the perfect home haunt decor. Combine different size and shape cages for a creepier look. Add moss, straw or faux leaves from a garden center or hobby store to cover the bottom of the cages and spray or hot glue some webs around the outside for a haunting, mis-kept look.

Sometimes the inhabitants escape their confines!

 A pair of small, white owl statuettes look out from a nest of straw and spider webs.

4

Cages can be fancy, plain, small or large. Variety is the key in this creature collection!!

5

5 Body parts, such as this creepy hand make a dramatic statement in a cage. What strange life must it have all its own to have to be locked in a cage?

6 Not all cages have to be big. These palm sized cages can be filled to the brim with colorful, plastic frogs or add a small, faux bird's nest with one large sized toad.

7 Realistic looking children's toys are perfect for the cage. The posed to strike, coiled snake is placed in a bed of dried Spanish moss with some faux bird's eggs.

6

You can never have too many toads!

2 This hand-made creature consists of a single bloodshot eye, some plastic fang teeth and faux fur.

3 Large, plastic bugs can be placed inside and outside cages for great effect.

4 Small stuffed, toy creatures, like this mini-werewolf look perfect hanging in a cage.

7

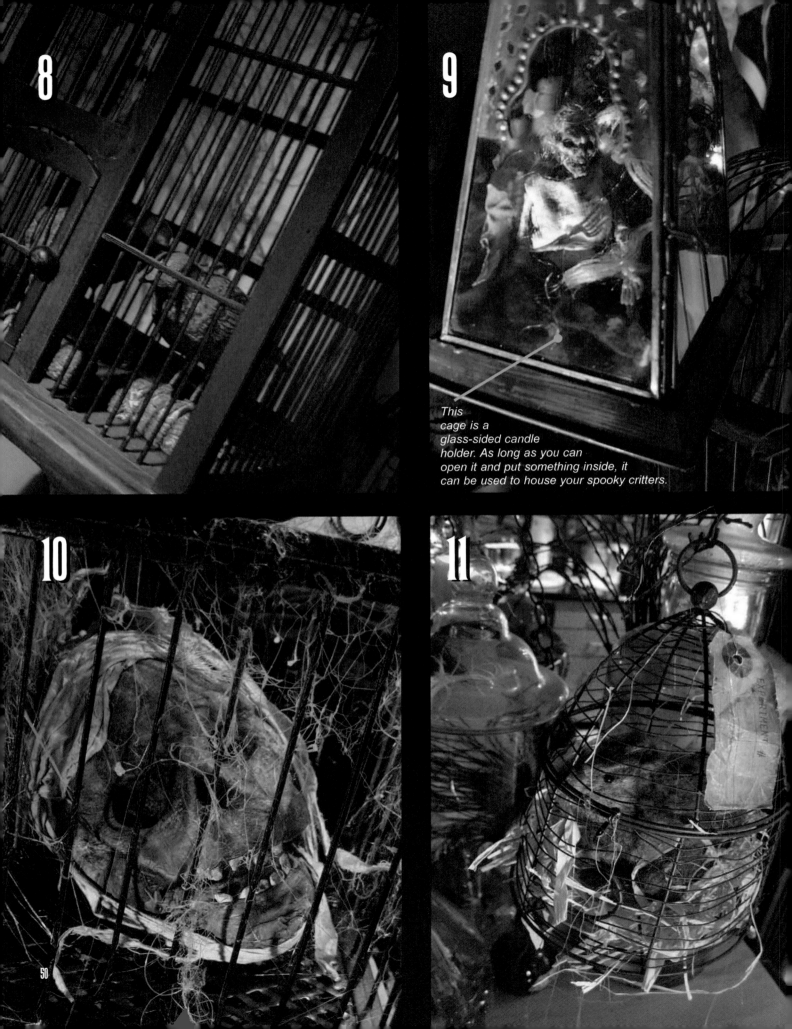

8

9

This cage is a glass-sided candle holder. As long as you can open it and put something inside, it can be used to house your spooky critters.

10

11

Think outside the "cage" for occupants to go inside. How about stone birds? The viewer may wonder if they could come to life at any moment...

Some caged beings may not have been well tended. This poor creature seems to have perished long ago, leaving its skeletal remains.

What devilish spell was cast upon this mummy's head? Add hot glue spider webs for aged look.

Realistic mouse in a nest of straw. Add old tags or labels to cages for mad-lab appearance.

Animated, children's toys, such as this baby dinosaur, which makes sounds, spits a venomous stream of water, and snaps at unwary fingers, are perfect for creature cages. Here, some faux fern leaves and moss covered branches were added to the cage for a more homey look. Don't forget a few severed fingers or bones as a warning to guests to keep their fingers out of reach!

Haunt Tips

Cages can be placed on tables or suspended from chains of various heights.

Drape a cage with a dark cloth or spider web cheese-cloth to partially conceal what it is inside

Battery operated Candles placed inside cages creates a spooky ambiance

Hang a group of creature cages close together, then spray with a hot glue spider webbing for an aged effect (*see Spooky Chandelier, page 28 for more details*). Draping some spider web cheese cloth would also work well.

Severed prop finger

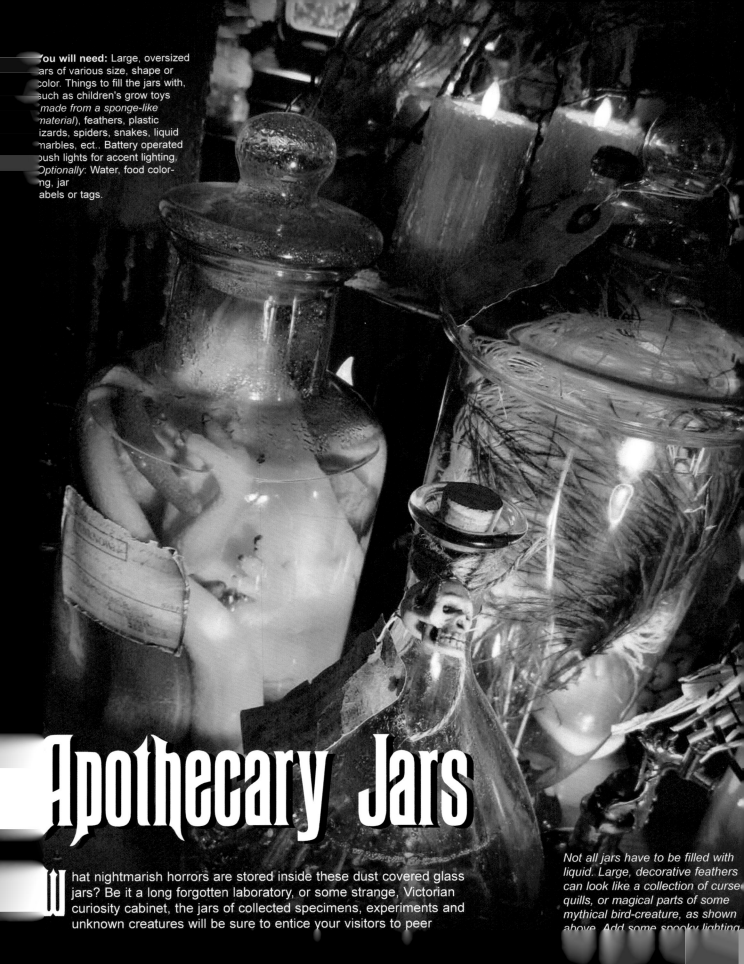

You will need: Large, oversized jars of various size, shape or color. Things to fill the jars with, such as children's grow toys (*made from a sponge-like material*), feathers, plastic lizards, spiders, snakes, liquid marbles, ect.. Battery operated push lights for accent lighting. *Optionally*: Water, food coloring, jar labels or tags.

Apothecary Jars

What nightmarish horrors are stored inside these dust covered glass jars? Be it a long forgotten laboratory, or some strange, Victorian curiosity cabinet, the jars of collected specimens, experiments and unknown creatures will be sure to entice your visitors to peer

Not all jars have to be filled with liquid. Large, decorative feathers can look like a collection of curse quills, or magical parts of some mythical bird-creature, as shown above. Add some spooky lighting

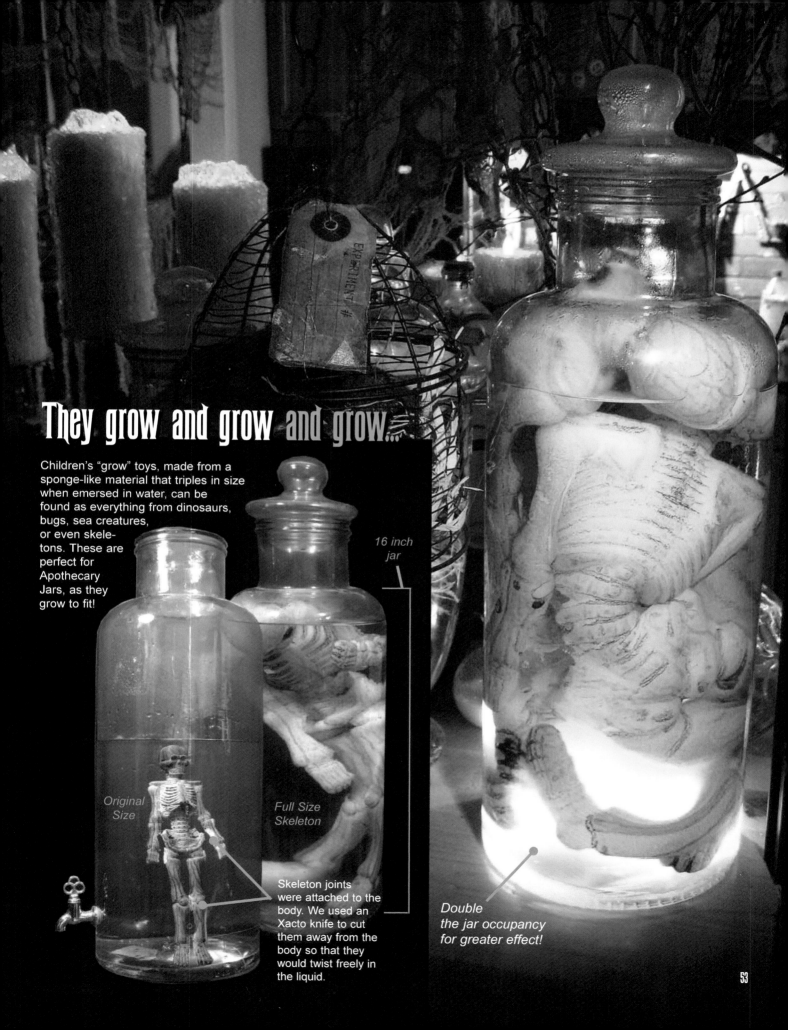

They grow and grow and grow...

Children's "grow" toys, made from a sponge-like material that triples in size when emersed in water, can be found as everything from dinosaurs, bugs, sea creatures, or even skeletons. These are perfect for Apothecary Jars, as they grow to fit!

16 inch jar

Original Size

Full Size Skeleton

Skeleton joints were attached to the body. We used an Xacto knife to cut them away from the body so that they would twist freely in the liquid.

Double the jar occupancy for greater effect!

53

The Strange Collection

1 Two giant, "grow" toy lizards of different colors, make a colorful display.

2 This apothecary jar is filled with Liquid Marbles, a decorative accent product. Add some small frogs, a few drops of green food coloring and a tad pole hatchery is created.

3 Two oversized snakes help to fill the jar space and double the creep factor with body parts twisting together in unnatural ways in too tight of a space! In the jar behind, is a collection of serpent eggs, *aka:* craft store bird eggs.

4 How about a baby dinosaur floating in abiotic fluid? A small, white push light behind the jar adds the perfect cinematic effect.

5 Just a drop or two of black food coloring in water partially conceals what is in this jar full of tentacles.

6 Yellow food coloring adds age to this slithering

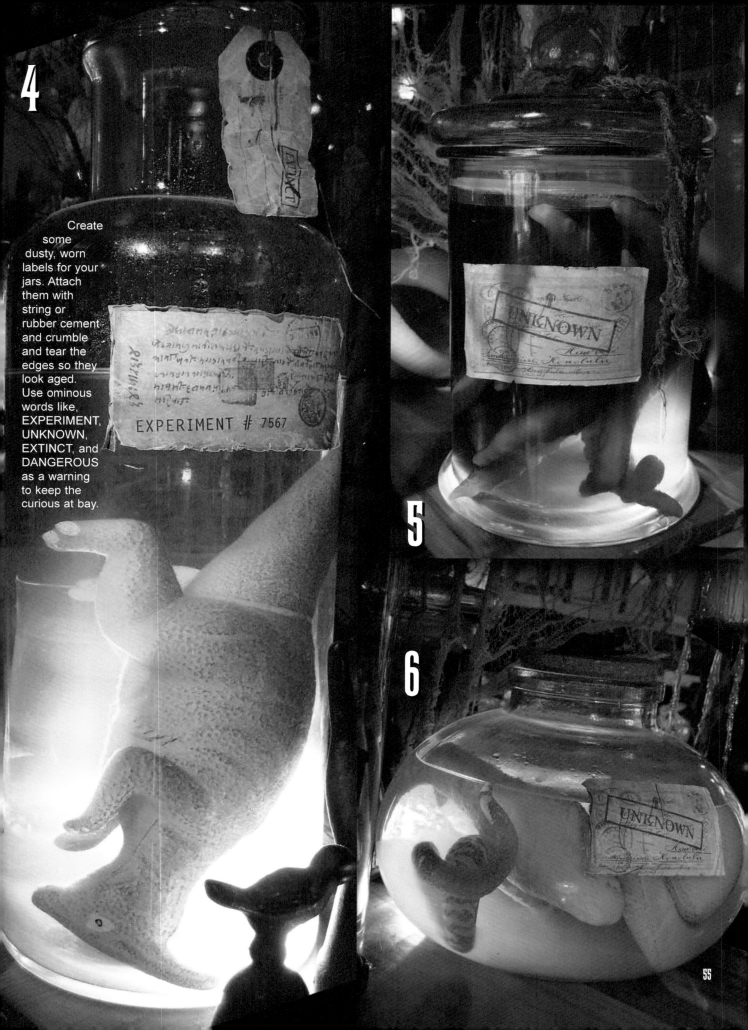

4

Create some dusty, worn labels for your jars. Attach them with string or rubber cement and crumble and tear the edges so they look aged. Use ominous words like, EXPERIMENT, UNKNOWN, EXTINCT, and DANGEROUS as a warning to keep the curious at bay.

EXPERIMENT # 7567

UNKNOWN

5

6

UNKNOWN

Cemetery Gate
with Gargoyle Columns

You will need: 5 pieces of 1x2 wood, 2x4 wood (*for extra support for column bases*), 8- 1'x4' wood planks (*for two columns*), 24 L brackets, 3 inch wood screws, 1 inch wood screws, wood glue, drill, 7/8 drill bit for cutting holes, jigsaw for cutting slots in the column sides, PVC cutter, 4 hinges, ½ PVC cut to various lengths, sand, several cans of black spray paint, black, brown, white craft paints, paint brush, sponge or cheesecloth for applying paint

I n book one of, *How To Haunt Your House*, we showed you how to create a cemetery fence. Here we take it a step further and create a cemetery gate with two gargoyle columns to go with it. The gargoyles here, were purchased props. Other props, such as urns with faux flowers, jack-o-lanterns, or lights could also be used. Simply add a top board to the columns and place whatever you want on top. Gate and Gargoyle Columns could also be used as a stand alone prop or at the entrance of a haunted crypt.

Top end
of column

1 Attach 4 planks of 1'x4'
together using 1 inch wood
screws and L brackets. Set
the four L brackets along the
bottom higher than where the 2x4
will be placed.
OPTIONAL: If creating a top for
the column, duplicate the 2x4 trim
around the top of the column.
Offset the position of the top L
brackets so the 2x4 will not go on
top of them. Then cut a piece of
1'x4' plank, or other scrap wood, to
fit on top of opening. Glue or
screw in to place.

Bottom end
of column

2 Measure out sections of 2x4
to fit around the base (and
top, if needed). Use the 3"
screws to attach to column.

3 If using a similar
prop that is hollow,
make sure the
prop will fit over
the column top.

4 Once your gate pieces are complete
(see pages 58-59), stand the columns
next to the gate ends. Mark out where
to place 2 pieces of 1x2 wood so they
can be attached to the gate end without overlapping the hinge hardware.

Wouldn't this
even look great
on it's own as a
gargoyle
pedestal?

See *How to Haunt Your House, Book One,* for how to create custom Fence Toppers that can also be used on the gate pieces.

Assembling the Gate

5 In order for the 1 inch wood screws not to stick out the backside of the 1x2 wood when attached to the hinges, glue two scrap pieces of 1x2 on the back of where the hinges will go. The pieces should be slightly longer than your hinge. Screw in the hinges leaving enough space for the L brackets shown in next step.

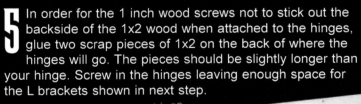

Scrap wood on back of gate hinge

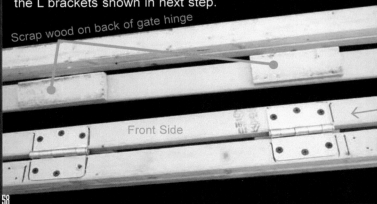

Front Side

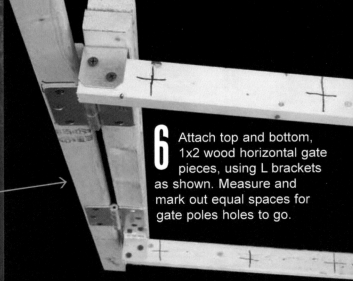

6 Attach top and bottom, 1x2 wood horizontal gate pieces, using L brackets as shown. Measure and mark out equal spaces for gate poles holes to go.

7 Use a 7/8 drill bit to cut holes for the PVC poles. Match the drilled holes, **top** and bottom for each gate section.

2 foot wide

2 foot wide

Decide whether to have your gates open in or out. These open forward. Turn the whole piece around to open outward

The height and width of your gate pieces will depend on your fence and column sizes.

8 Measure out a length of PVC from the outside gate edge to the highest point on the inner gate section. Use 1 inch wood screws to attach.

23 inches wide

9 Use a jigsaw to cut out the slots in the column sides so that two pieces of 1x2 can slide through. These will be used to attach the column to both one gate section and a section of fencing on the opposite side. Pre-drill pilot holes for the wood screws in both ends so the wood will not split when attaching to the gate pieces.

37 inches high

48 inches high

24 inches wide

22 inches high

10 Cut various lengths of PVC poles to fit in the holes. Use wood screws to attach the top of the PVC poles to the curved PVC piece.

Painting the Columns

11 Mix base color (*in this case, gray*) with sand. The sand will provide texture and help match the look of the gargoyle statues. Cover the entire columns and let dry.

Use just enough sand to give the paint some texture.

12 Using a sponge or cheesecloth, dab small amounts of black, white and brown, craft paint over the base coat for a variegated stone look. Let dry.

Simple changes to store-bought props can really add more drama to the pieces.

Before

After

A Little Extra...

13 To give the gargoyles more contrast use a paint brush to apply black, craft paint mixed with a generous amount of water to various parts of the statue. Let the paint run down, filling in cracks and crevices on its own for a more natural weathered look. Let dry.

14 Spray paint all the gate pieces black. Let dry. Attach gates to column wood supports with screws. Add Fence Toppers (See *Book 1, How To Haunt Your House*), snake, moss or spiders web draped over the bars and the project is complete.

The Bubbling Cauldron

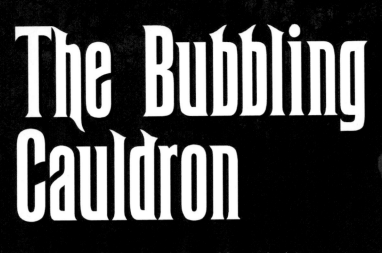

This overflowing concoction of fog and mist are sure to make the visitors wonder what foul ingredients lie within. This bubbling cauldron could be used indoors or outside. Water may splash out of the cauldron, so make sure electric plugs, outlets or non-waterproof items are out of reach.

You will need: 1 plastic cauldron, 1 or more pond misters with or without built-in lights, plastic bowl that will fit inside of cauldron, water, pond mister splash shield (optional), red or yellow string lights (*optional*)

1. Securely place a bowl for water inside the caldron. Place one or more pond misters in the bowl. Cut a hole in the back of the caldron to pull the mister cords through. Take the cords over the inner bowl edge, though the inside of the cauldron and out the cut hole.

Tip: Add a plastic spider or small Styrofoam skull to the top of the splash guard with a small dab of hot glue to conceal it.

2. Fill the bowl with enough water to cover the misters. Use splash guards over the misters, if needed. Turn on misters and test. You may need to raise the inner bowl up if the mister fog does not roll over the cauldron edge when turned on.

3. A converted pedestal birdbath becomes a fire pit for the cauldron. Beneath the cauldron, place a collection of sticks and red or yellow string lights to resemble a wood burning fire. Arrange the setting with posed props around the cauldron such as a witch or a couple of skeletons as shown here.

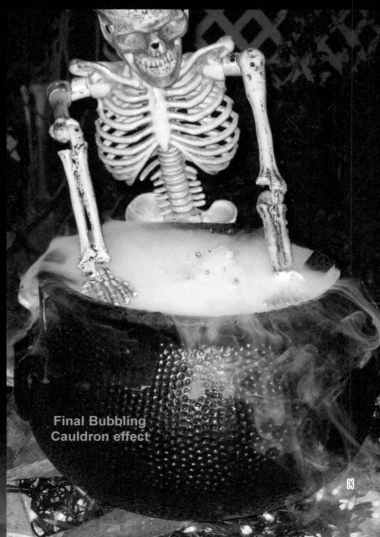

Final Bubbling Cauldron effect

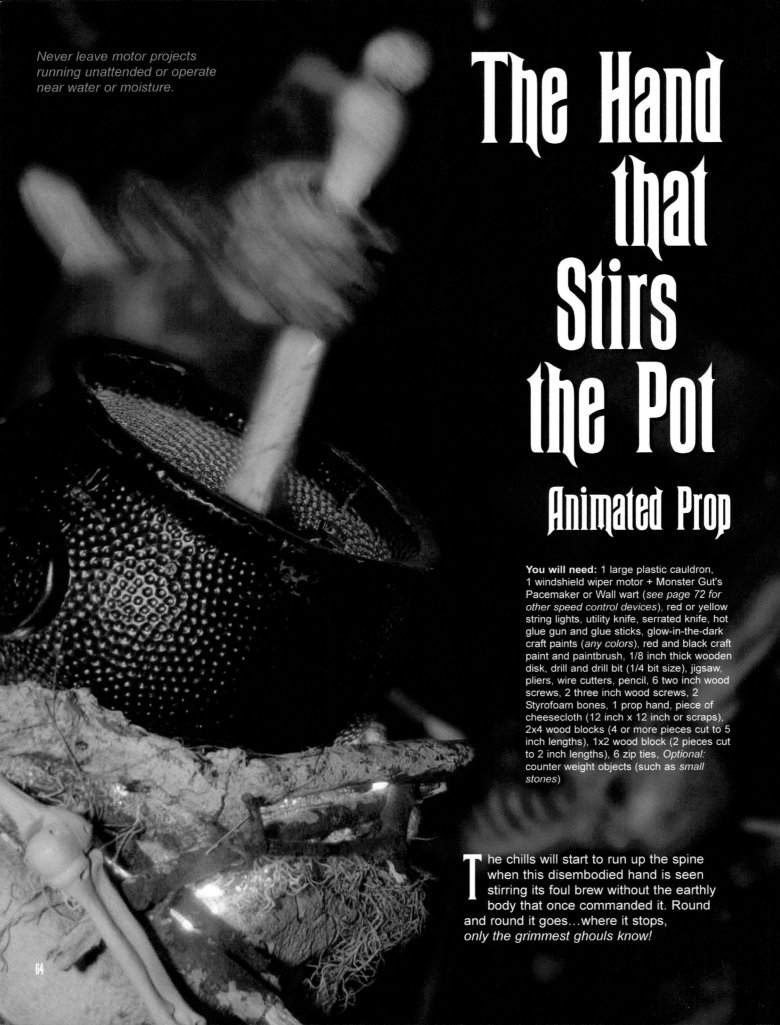

Never leave motor projects running unattended or operate near water or moisture.

The Hand that Stirs the Pot
Animated Prop

You will need: 1 large plastic cauldron, 1 windshield wiper motor + Monster Gut's Pacemaker or Wall wart (*see page 72 for other speed control devices*), red or yellow string lights, utility knife, serrated knife, hot glue gun and glue sticks, glow-in-the-dark craft paints (*any colors*), red and black craft paint and paintbrush, 1/8 inch thick wooden disk, drill and drill bit (1/4 bit size), jigsaw, pliers, wire cutters, pencil, 6 two inch wood screws, 2 three inch wood screws, 2 Styrofoam bones, 1 prop hand, piece of cheesecloth (12 inch x 12 inch or scraps), 2x4 wood blocks (4 or more pieces cut to 5 inch lengths), 1x2 wood block (2 pieces cut to 2 inch lengths), 6 zip ties, *Optional: counter weight objects (such as small stones)*

T he chills will start to run up the spine when this disembodied hand is seen stirring its foul brew without the earthly body that once commanded it. Round and round it goes…where it stops, *only the grimmest ghouls know!*

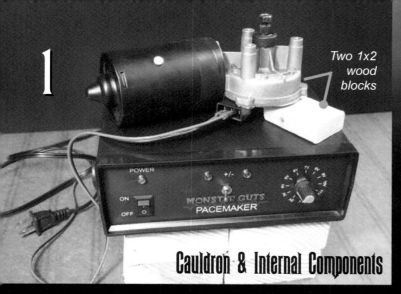

Two 1x2 wood blocks

Cauldron & Internal Components

1 Hot glue two 1x2 pieces of wood to bottom of motor to keep it level. Stack all components and as many 2x4 pieces of wood necessary to achieve a height just below the inner lip of the cauldron when assembled.

2 Use the 3 inch screws to attach 2 sets of 2 wood blocks as shown. Attach 2 zip ties on each set. These will be used later to attach motor to the blocks.

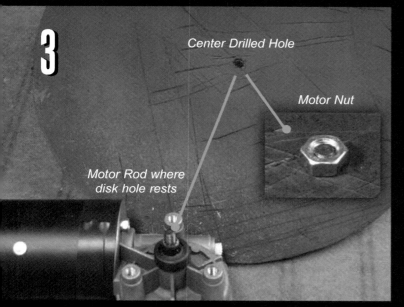

Center Drilled Hole

Motor Nut

Motor Rod where disk hole rests

3 Measure 1 inch smaller than across the inside of the cauldron just inside the lip. Use this as the diameter to cut out a 1/8 thick wooden disk. Drill a 1/4 inch hole in the center. Paint the top of the disk black. Let dry.

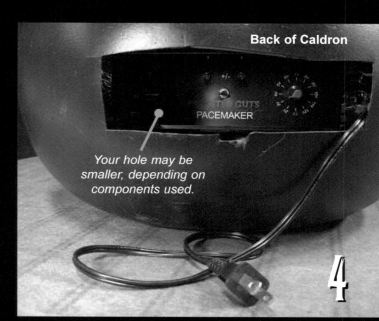

Back of Caldron

Your hole may be smaller, depending on components used.

4 Determine what size hole will need to be cut in the back to access the inside controls. Cut hole using a utility knife. Pull any plugs through this hole.

With the motor lower than the cauldron edge, add the string lights around the stack.

Zip tie motor to block straps.

Remove the motor nut and slip the disk over the end. Re-attach the nut. Test to see if the disk has enough room to freely rotate and allow light to show through from the inside.

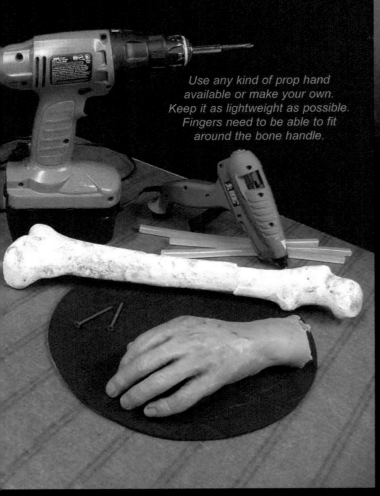

Use any kind of prop hand available or make your own. Keep it as lightweight as possible. Fingers need to be able to fit around the bone handle.

Assembling the Bone Spoon and Hand Prop

7 Remove the motor nut and wooden disk. Set aside. Cut one end of the Styrofoam bone so it will sit flush against the wood disk using a serrated knife.

8 Use wire cutters to remove the Styrofoam bone wire.

7

8

9 Use a pencil to trace out a position close to the center of the disk for the bone.

Mark two points for screws. Pre-drill two holes. From the underside of the wood disk screw two 2 inch, wood screws.

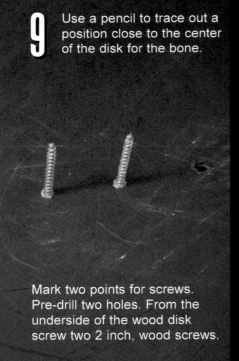

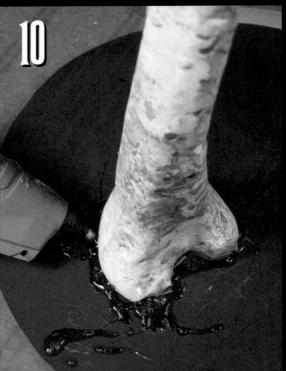

10 Carefully, push the Styrofoam bone down onto the screws. Hot glue around bone to hold firmly in place.

11 Run additional hot glue trails around the disk for texture as shown. Let cool.

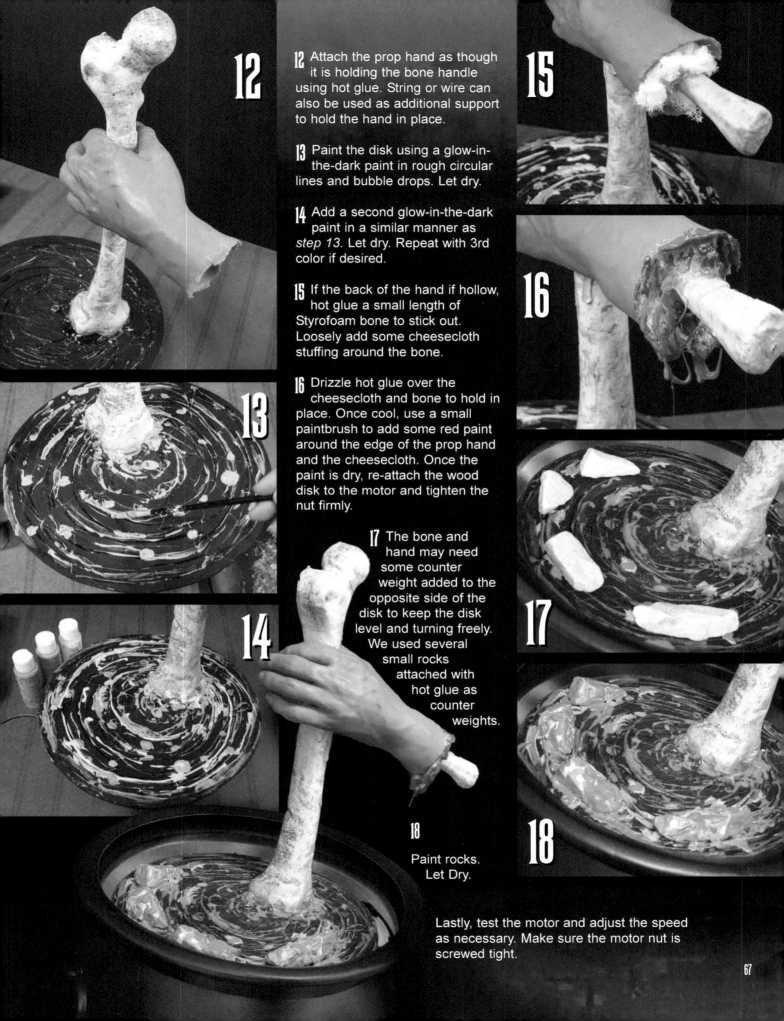

12 Attach the prop hand as though it is holding the bone handle using hot glue. String or wire can also be used as additional support to hold the hand in place.

13 Paint the disk using a glow-in-the-dark paint in rough circular lines and bubble drops. Let dry.

14 Add a second glow-in-the-dark paint in a similar manner as *step 13*. Let dry. Repeat with 3rd color if desired.

15 If the back of the hand if hollow, hot glue a small length of Styrofoam bone to stick out. Loosely add some cheesecloth stuffing around the bone.

16 Drizzle hot glue over the cheesecloth and bone to hold in place. Once cool, use a small paintbrush to add some red paint around the edge of the prop hand and the cheesecloth. Once the paint is dry, re-attach the wood disk to the motor and tighten the nut firmly.

17 The bone and hand may need some counter weight added to the opposite side of the disk to keep the disk level and turning freely. We used several small rocks attached with hot glue as counter weights.

18 Paint rocks. Let Dry.

Lastly, test the motor and adjust the speed as necessary. Make sure the motor nut is screwed tight.

Tomb Turner
Animated Prop

You will need: <u>PVC parts:</u> 1 cap, 2 elbows, 1 Tee,
¾ inch PVC pieces in lengths of 1 inch, 2 inch,
5.5 inch, 9.5 inch, 17 inch. and 28 inch
<u>Metal parts:</u> 3 large washers with ¼ hole, 2 bolts
with nuts, 3 large eye hooks, 2 flat metal strong
ties (12 inch), one 1/8 thick flat metal (10 inch),
One 2x4 metal brace
2x4 wood 28 inch length
2'x2' piece of wood for base
Wiper blade motor with speed control
component (*Wall wart used here*)
<u>Prop figure:</u> cheap plastic skeleton, two
prop hands, Styrofoam skull, face
mask, torn shirt and jeans,
Styrofoam bones,
Shredded rope hair
Craft paints (black, blue,
and gray)
Hot glue gun and sticks
Tan pantyhose,
size small
Tombstone
Wood screws
PVC glue
Carpet
glue

*This Tomb
Turner can be
tucked away in
a corner
indoors or used
outdoors in
good weather.*

When the undead start moving in a cemetery…
people usually start running. This undead
scare-actor is relatively harmless and moves
only enough to raise a few goose bumps.
He turns from side to side, sitting atop his
tombstone, casting his dead stare at those who
pass by. Made from scratch, this animated prop is
created with a few, easy to assemble items and a

Skin & Bones

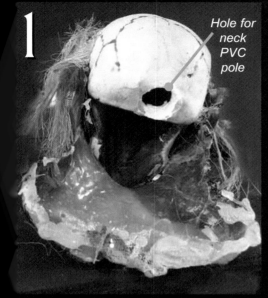

Hole for neck PVC pole

1 Use whatever prop parts you have on hand for your tomb turner. You could use an entire plastic skeleton, or bits and parts, as we have. This head uses a Styrofoam skull with a hole cut in the base for the PVC neck pole to insert into.

2 Cut parts away from the head "skin" so the Styrofoam skull shows through. Any latex store-bought mask could be used for the "skin". First, cut away parts in a similar way shown. Next, hot glue a few areas under the remaining mask to hold in place. Leave the rest free floating so it resembles loose skin separating from bone. If needed, use blue and gray craft paints to give the skin a "dead" look. Last, unravel a rope to create hair strands. Hot glue hair to head in random areas. Allow the hair to stick out for wild look.

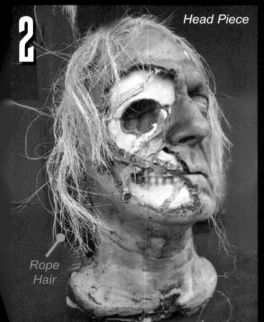

Head Piece

Rope Hair

3 Use a utility knife to cut some gaps between the rib bones of a plastic skeleton rib cage. Coat all the plastic bones with carpet glue. Insert both arms into a pair of pantyhose legs. The waist section will go over the rib cage. Cut a hole for the neck to go through. Trim away any excess hose. While the glue is still tacky, cut random slits in the hose, and roll back the edges. It should look like remnants of muscle clinging to bone.

4 Optionally, create some hot glue "skin" patches. *To create:* hot glue a rough, patch-sized amount onto parchment paper. Let cool. Remove and paint with craft paints. Attach patch to bone with hot glue in random areas.

5 Leave some hose strands pulled away, or hanging, from the bone to look like sinew. Bones should still be able to bend and pose as needed.

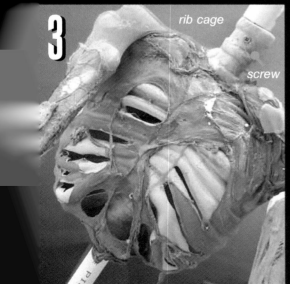

rib cage

screw

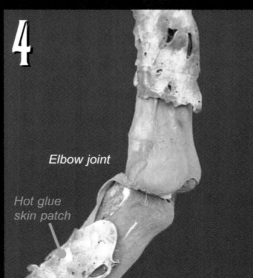

Elbow joint

Hot glue skin patch

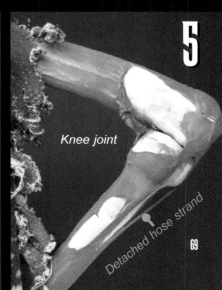

Knee joint

Detached hose strand

Dressing the Tomb Turner

Get creative in dressing your tomb turner. It could be a male or female. Thrift stores or garage sales are perfect for finding old clothes to use. They can be covered in freshly dug up "grave" dirt (*garden dirt*), "blood" splattered (*red paint*) or just torn and tattered. The choice is yours.

1 Corpsify a pair of jeans or old pants, using a spray bottle and bleach. Spray in random areas, then cut holes for leg bones to show through. Shred the pant leg ends. A scrap of cloth is used to tie the jeans around the hip bones.

2 Cut a hole in the base of the jeans and the plastic hip bone section. Place the hip bone inside the jeans and slide over the PVC pipe *before* attaching the upper body/rib cage section. The hips will "sit" on top of a tombstone that leans against the vertical 2x4 wood. Screw the upper body/rib cage section to it's PVC pole.

3 We substituted a plastic leg with some Styrofoam bones on one leg, as well as the feet. We also used prop hands instead of plastic ones.

4 A cotton, button down shirt was shredded and torn almost completely with the strands left to hang off the shoulders. This allowed most of the body bones to show though.

Never leave motor projects running unattended or operate near water or moisture.

5 Assemble the motor and Inner Workings, as shown on *page 71*. PVC glue the "Elbow" and "Tee" PVC pieces. Once the motor is turned on, the tomb turner upper body will turn from side to side. Adjust the speed till desired effect is achieved. We used a 3Volt setting for a creepy, slow movement.

Drill two holes through one end of the PVC for the bolt and nut. It should be loose fitting and allow the PVC and metal to turn.

Inner Workings

3/4 PVC 5.5 inch

PVC Elbow

PVC glue this connection

Plastic rib cage

3/4 PVC 17 inch

PVC elbow

Plastic Hip Bone

PVC glue this connection

2x4 wood 28 inch

3/4 PVC 28 inch

PVC "Tee"

3/4 PVC 9.5 inch

3/4 PVC 2 inch

PVC Cap

2'x2' wood base

Eye hooks hold the PVC in place, but still allow PVC to rotate

screw metal brace into 2x4 and 2x2 base

2' x 2' wooden base painted black.

You will need to put the pants on the hips *before* assembling the rib cage section and upper

Space out and center the 3 Eye Hooks along the 2x4 wood.

Connect PVC, metal ties and bolts using a similar layout shown here.

PVC glue this connection

Motor rod rotates 360 degrees, turning the first metal strip. Be sure the rod nut is tight.

Wall Wart connects to the Quick Connect wire.

Use a 3/4 PVC 1 inch piece to separate the metal arms. This section needs to be able to rotate.

A Wall Wart allows multi-speed control over the motor.

See *page 70* for information on using wiper motors and controlling the speed of the prop.

71

Motor Speed Controllers

Being able to control the speed of motor props has always been a challenge for the home haunter. Being mechanically challenged ourselves, we needed easy ways to do this. This chapter shows three ways to control or reduce a wiper blade motor speed.

How much speed reduction needed always depends on the motor project and experimentation. Some props might look better at faster, jerky motions, while others, the effect calls for slower, smoother motions. Always use caution when using motors in the home haunt setting. Make sure moving parts are

clear of obstacles, people and pets. Never leave a motor project running unsupervised. If you smell anything burning or melting, quickly unplug the devise.

There are many great online resources for creating simple motor project which move in a variety of ways. Do a search for *"wiper motor props"* and find out more.

Motor rod, washer and removable Nut

12VDC Wiper Blade Motor
Motor rod rotates when motor is on.

Pacemaker comes with its own quick connect wire

POWER

+/-

7V   8V
6V   9V
5V   10V
4V   11V
3V   12V
2V   1V

ON

MONSTER GUTS
PACEMAKER

OFF

The Pacemaker by Monster Guts

This plug and play method is versatile and filled with options. It not only allows you to control the speed with 12 speed settings, but also to change the direction the motor spins. Plug the wire connectors into the motor and plug in the power cord and it is ready to go.

Motor Connect detail

Wall Wart

Wall Wart (Power Supply) is an oversized, electrical device power plug. This universal AC Adapter also has 3 to 12 volt settings for controlling the motor speed. 3V is great for slow, even movement. 12V is the normal wiper motor speed, but can be too fast for some projects. This component can be found online or in the most stores' electronics department near cell phone chargers.

Connects
to motor

Connects to
power supply

Quick
Connect
attached to
motor

Quick Connect
then attaches to
power supply
jack

Quick Connect by Monster Guts

This handy component makes connecting the wiper motor to the speed controllers very easy. One end plugs into the motor wire port, the other into the speed controllers plug.

See **Tomb Turner**, *page 68* and
The Hand that Stirs the Pot, *page 64*
for two motor projects in this book.

5 Volt Power Supply by Monster Guts

If you only need to slow your motor down a little, you can use a 5 Volt 5 Amp Power Supply which can reduce a wiper motor's RPMs by 60%.

Grave Ghosts

You will need: 1 inch and 2 inch cell chicken wire by the roll, 24 inches wide, available at most hardware stores, wire cutters, lots of semi-transparent fabric (*old curtains are perfect*), 3 or more yards of white cheesecloth, "S" hook painted black (*one for each hanging ghost*), scissors, thin wire (*or save the wire that wraps the chicken wire rolls*), mannequin head or small head sized ball, 1 wire hanger, and protective gloves. *Optional:* white netting fabric which will glow in Blacklight

24x24
1 inch cell

1 Cut 24" length of chicken wire
Chicken wire sold in 1 or 2 inch cell sizes

Wear protective gloves when working with wire. Ends are *SHARP!*

2 Bend chicken wire over head form. Exact shape in not needed.

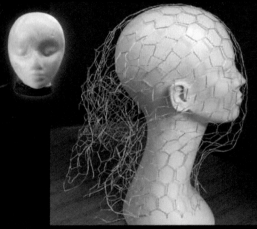

3 Bend the excess towards the back. Form a rough Neck shape.

The gray lady, the lady in blue, the transparent, silhouette on the widow's walk... we've all heard tales of those that refuse to leave this earthly realm. They wait and watch. They wander endlessly though the graveyard haze, unaware of the frightened gazes of the living who have glimpsed their unearthly forms. These lightweight, ghosts are right at home as props for Halloween or the home haunt cemetery. Free-standing figures or half figures can be easily built with just a few simple materials.

4 Remove head form and reshape as needed. Set wire head aside for later.

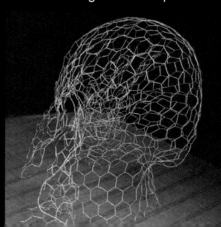

74

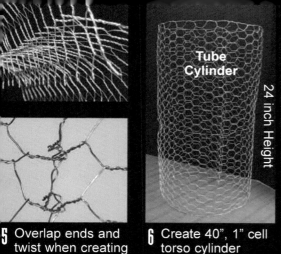

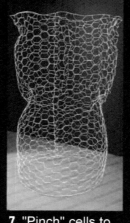

Tube Cylinder

24 inch Height

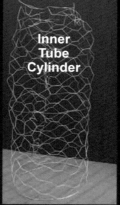

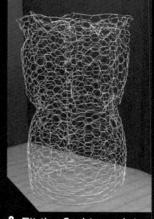

Inner Tube Cylinder

5 Overlap ends and twist when creating cylinder form seams.

6 Create 40", 1" cell torso cylinder

7 "Pinch" cells to form waist and shoulder points

8 Create 2nd slightly smaller 2" cell torso cylinder.

9 Fit the 2nd torso into the first to add extra support.

Form 2 cylinders for arms.

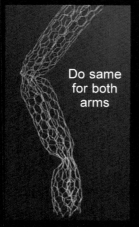

Do same for both arms

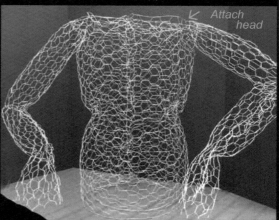

Attach head

10 Cut 32" length, 1" cell. Cut in half lengthways.

11 Pinch at elbow and wrist joints as shown.

12 Twist small wire at elbow joint to hold bent position.

13 Use small wires to attach both arms to torso. Twist wire ends of head base to top of figure and shoulder area.

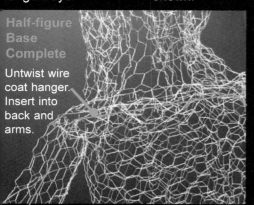

Half-figure Base Complete

Untwist wire coat hanger. Insert into back and arms.

Continue from here for Full-figure

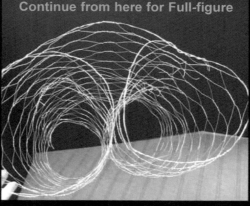

14 Use small wires to attach head form to top of torso. Insert wire clothes hanger into back & arms for support. Stop here for half figure wire base.

15 Roll 4' length of 2" cells into shape as shown. Twist cell ends to back to hold shape. Make two.

16 Wrap 42" 1" cell piece around the two pieces made. Twist ends at seam to hold.

17 Create tube with 1" cell, cut in half. Place finished edges down.

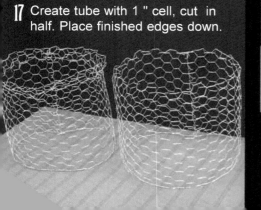

18 Use wire to attach one piece to bottom of torso and the 2nd to the backside, slightly squished.

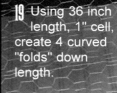

19 Using 36 inch length, 1" cell, create 4 curved "folds" down length.

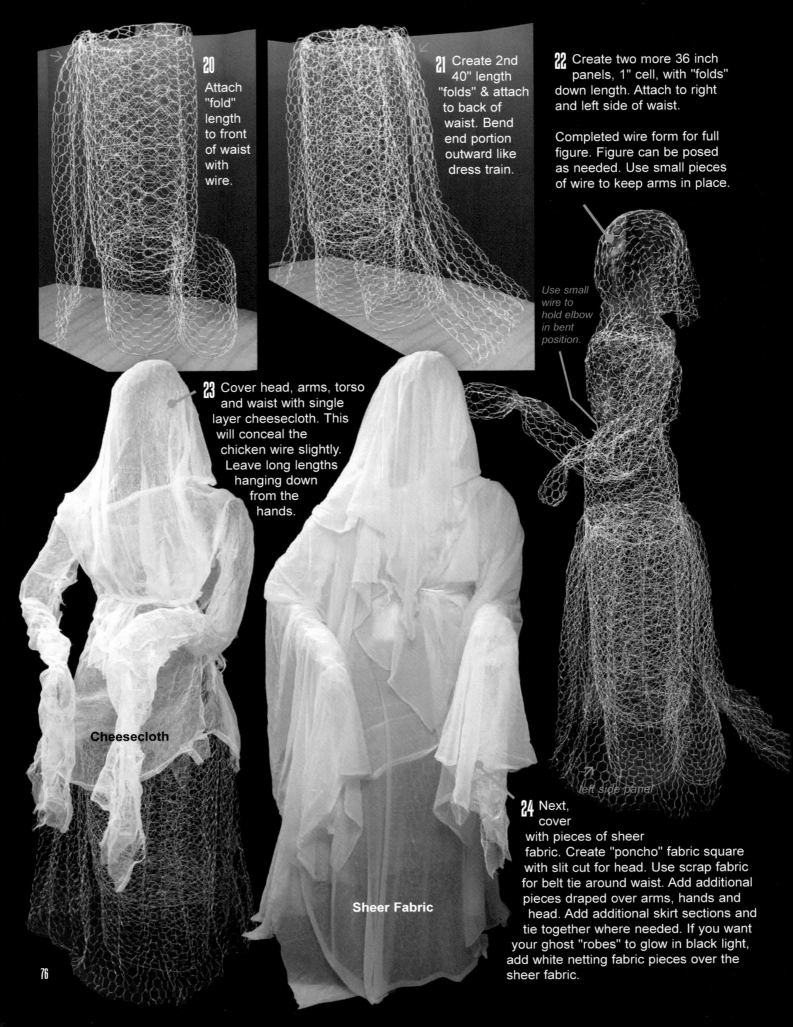

20 Attach "fold" length to front of waist with wire.

21 Create 2nd 40" length "folds" & attach to back of waist. Bend end portion outward like dress train.

22 Create two more 36 inch panels, 1" cell, with "folds" down length. Attach to right and left side of waist.

Completed wire form for full figure. Figure can be posed as needed. Use small pieces of wire to keep arms in place.

Use small wire to hold elbow in bent position.

23 Cover head, arms, torso and waist with single layer cheesecloth. This will conceal the chicken wire slightly. Leave long lengths hanging down from the hands.

left side panel

Cheesecloth

Sheer Fabric

24 Next, cover with pieces of sheer fabric. Create "poncho" fabric square with slit cut for head. Use scrap fabric for belt tie around waist. Add additional pieces draped over arms, hands and head. Add additional skirt sections and tie together where needed. If you want your ghost "robes" to glow in black light, add white netting fabric pieces over the sheer fabric.

Half-figure

Half-figures are light enough to be suspended with string or strong fishing line. Black, garden planter stakes can also be used to hold the half-figures up off the ground and appear to float at night as shown here.

These Half and Full figures can appear semi-transparent with the addition of lighting or be suspended for a floating ghost effect.

25 Once all the fabric has been added, cut holes and long tattered end pieces similar to figures shown.

Here a small lantern is attached to arm with wire and a battery operated candle added.

Full-figure

Full-figures can be placed outdoors in your home haunt setting. Being lightweight, they are easy to move to a new location as needed. Use additional stakes, as needed, to keep from being blown over.

Be sure **not** to place hot lights near the ghost's fabric body.

Making An Entrance

Leering from lampposts and reaching out from banisters, trick-or-treaters and party guests must make their way past this group of posable skeletons before reaching the door. When it comes to creating your home haunt entrance, a few props, some lights, and loads of spider webs (*cheesecloth or bag variety*) can go a long way in achieving a haunted appearance. The entrance is the first thing guests will see.

How this setting was created: *Blue
and yellow shop lights were used to
light the area. The lights were securely placed at low angles and pointed
up to create dramatic shadows. Red,
flicker bulbs were added to two lamp
posts. Faux moss was hung off the
roof edge over the doorway. Yards of
cheesecloth spider web was hung
from various places and moved slightly in the breeze. Dry leaves from the
yard were collected and strewn over
the deck to the door entrance.*

*Above: Just inside the door, as seen
through the glass above, stands a
dimly lit figure prop. Will he have a
trick, or treat, for those brave
enough to make it to the door?*

*Right: A pair of store-bought,
prop gargoyles stand on either
side of the door. Stretch spider
webbing, from a bag, were
used here, creating a thick,
layered look of cobwebs.*

Setting the Stage:
Inside the Haunted House

Walking into the haunted house… This thought conjures up strange emotions of both instinctive fear and a pulling curiosity. We want to know what is inside, but don't want to look. Our pounding heart drowns out any disembodied, whispered voices we might possibly hear. Our whole body is tensed to turn and run, yet we walk on, deeper into the dark rooms and ominous hallways. A fearful thought slips through– *Will I make it out alive?* The last occupant didn't…

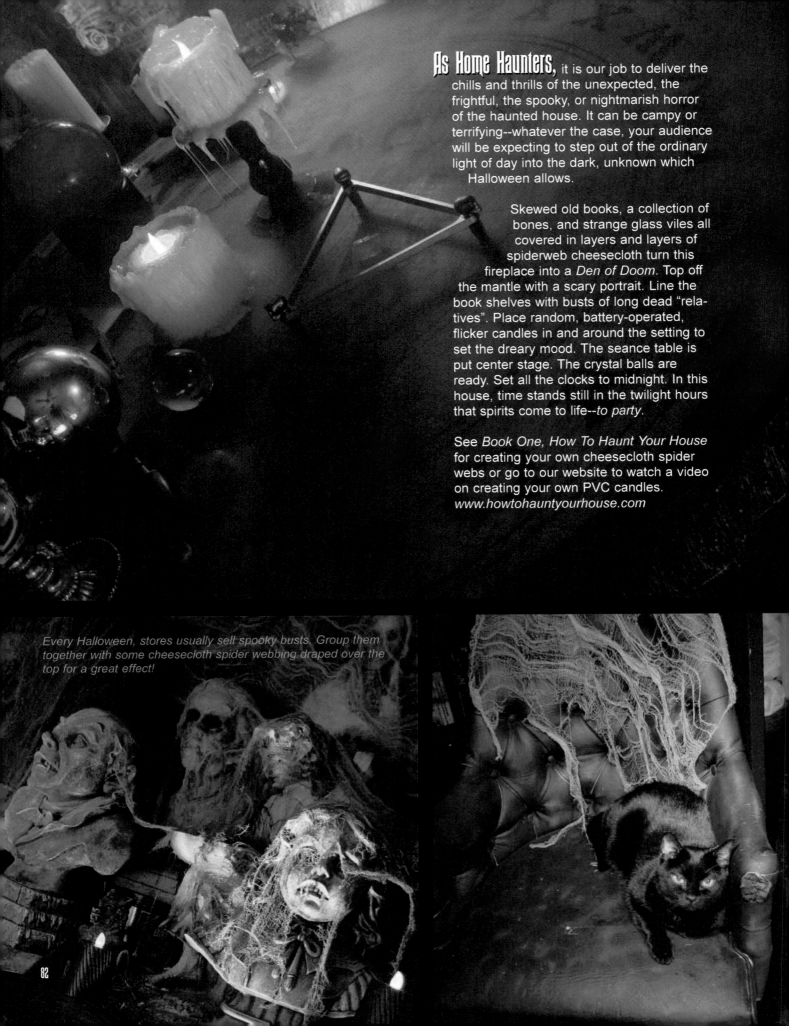

As Home Haunters, it is our job to deliver the chills and thrills of the unexpected, the frightful, the spooky, or nightmarish horror of the haunted house. It can be campy or terrifying--whatever the case, your audience will be expecting to step out of the ordinary light of day into the dark, unknown which Halloween allows.

Skewed old books, a collection of bones, and strange glass viles all covered in layers and layers of spiderweb cheesecloth turn this fireplace into a *Den of Doom*. Top off the mantle with a scary portrait. Line the book shelves with busts of long dead "relatives". Place random, battery-operated, flicker candles in and around the setting to set the dreary mood. The seance table is put center stage. The crystal balls are ready. Set all the clocks to midnight. In this house, time stands still in the twilight hours that spirits come to life--*to party*.

See *Book One, How To Haunt Your House* for creating your own cheesecloth spider webs or go to our website to watch a video on creating your own PVC candles. *www.howtohauntyourhouse.com*

Every Halloween, stores usually sell spooky busts. Group them together with some cheesecloth spider webbing draped over the top for a great effect!

Custom made Witches' bottles along with an assortment of glass containers, old books, spider web cheesecloth, prop bones, flicker light candles, and plastic bugs and spiders turn an ordinary kitchen into the Witches' pantry. Who can guess what potions are brewed here, or what spells might be cast on an unsuspecting guest?

Larger props or scare-actors can be placed inside the haunted house. Dark corners, empty niches, ends of halls—all can be occupied by ghouls, mummies, and vampire bats. Even if they never move, your guests will still imagine they can.

Keep the lighting dim. Add yellow or blue bulbs to lamps. Set a lamp on the floor instead of a table top. Add a Blacklight over a door. Place lights behind colored, glass props. All of these things change the look the room and add a sense of drama and shadow. As always, be careful of any fire hazards with lights and don't place items in walkways where someone could trip.

Notice!
To all Trick-or-Treaters,
Ghouls & Goblins—
You are Invited

to Tour the

HAUNTED
CEMETERY
on Halloween Night

to see Spooky Thrills and

Ghostly Visitations

among
the Mitchell Tombstones!

The Cemetery

Every haunted house should have a haunted cemetery. It can be a small family plot with a just few gravestones, or a larger walk through with untold number of restless spirits lingering around row upon row of ancient graves.

These pages offer a glimpse of what once was… a memory of Halloween's past. We hope a chill runs up your spine, and your hair stands of end, and more than once, you will glance over your shoulder at the unknown sounds in the night. Listen. Listen carefully for that child-like voice inside to say, *"It's Halloween time again…"*

A cemetery fence keeps our guests at a safe distance from the props and special effects and lighted Jack-o-lanterns help light the way. At one end, a glowing bride, quite literally lights up the night with Blacklight and a white, fabric netting bride's dress. At her side a host of skeletons stand among the tombstones. Fellow spirits, *or unfortunate grooms?*

Other Resources

For Wiper Motors and speed control components:
www.monsterguts.com Wiper blade motors, quick connects, power supplies, and The Pacemaker (for motor speed control)- they know what the home haunter needs and makes our lives so much easier!

Wall Wart (AC Adapter) with variable volts, can be found doing online searches for *Universal AC Adapter Power Supply* or from electronics departments where cell phone chargers are located.

For more cool Halloween props, special effects and costumes:
www.terrorsyndicate.com, www.scarefactory.com, www.frightcatalog.com, www.darkimaginings.com

www.halloweenpropmaster.com
The resource for home haunt DVDs and tutorials.

Some of the best home haunter forums:
www.hauntspace.com, www.halloween-l.com, www.halloweenforum.com, www.homehauntersassociation.com www.garageofevilnetwork.com www.hauntforum.com

Halloween websites, magazines, and webcast:
www.halloweenalliance.com,www.myscaryhalloween.com, www.homehauntnews.com, www.hauntcast.net

Halloween music:
www.inaworldmusic.net, www.midnightsyndicate.com

Drywall Compound, PVC Pipe, Paver Sand, Styrofoam should all be found in any major hardware store.

Halloween Props and Special FX Each year most major retail stores carry some sort of Halloween product displays of the latest props and special effects. As you are making your rounds for new additions to your collection, be sure to check out the craft and fabric stores at the same time. They also carry Halloween items. Don't forget the after Halloween clearance sales. This is a great way to add to your next year's prop arsenal without spending a whole lot of money. If you feel like shopping all year long for Halloween...there are many online shops devoted to Halloween. Doing a search for Halloween prop will get you started. One great resource is http://www.frightcatalog.com/

Cheesecloth can be purchased from most fabric stores. Some stores will sell it by the yard. Online searches for *fabric cheesecloth* will show many online resources for purchasing cheesecloth by the yard. One site example: http://www.hancockfabrics.com

Credits

Font credits: Ravenscroft font was originally conceived and drawn by Tim McKenny, then refined and developed by Justin Callaghan http://www.mickeyavenue.com.

Photos by Shawn and Lynne Mitchell. All projects in this book were used by Shawn and Lynne Mitchell for their Halloween home haunt, *The Mitchell Cemetery*.

Index

How To Haunt Your House

How To Haunt Your House - Book 1 - *Let the Haunting Begin...*

If you'd like to raise the coffin lid a little higher this year—check out these projects and tips in the book, **How To Haunt Your House**. Turn your usual Halloween bash into something really hair-raising this year! Over 300 color photos of step-by-step projects and inspirational photos.

The book is coming soon. Please email the authors here, if you would like to be informed as soon as it is available.

PREVIEW ENTIRE BOOK (click or drag corners to turn pages)

Hit play to view
BOOK REVIEW VIDEO

The Library

Shop for our latest books, artwork and T-shirts! All books can be

The Book Reviews

People are already talking about *How To Haunt Your House!* Advance copies of the book were sent out to haunt industry professionals and the reviews came back with overwhelming enthusiaim. Please feel free to send your own reviews. We want to know what you think and how we can improve for book two already in progress. Just send us an email.

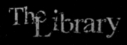

VISIT US AT
WWW.HOWTOHAUNTYOURHOUSE.COM

Thank You!

We would like to thank the following people for seeing us through our first and second books for, *How to Haunt Your House*. Without your help and encouragement we would not have accomplished it. Huge thanks to: Paul Venturella (aka: Propmaster) the maestro of all the home haunters. His DVD collections are what unites the home haunters from around the world and let so many share in the experience, even when we don't get to see it firsthand. Thanks to Chris Baker and the rest of the cast of Hauntcast.net: Johnny Thunder, Shellhawk, Dr. Morbius and Revenant, as well as Dirk Bergmann from HomeHaunter.de magazine for interviewing us and promoting our first book. To PropMaster, Chris Baker G-Host of Hauntcast.net, Pete Henderson of hauntspace.com, HauntStyle.com, Chris Molnar of Halloweenalliance.com and the Home Haunters Association Team for their glowing reviews of *How to Haunt Your House, Book Two*. Special thanks goes to Ron Quijano for once again giving the book a once over with an editorial eye. Thank you for the trio of awards we now have to show off-with the *Haunt X Award, Best Yard Haunt 2007, The Haunters Video Award Best Video Production 2009*, and *The "Propmaster" Award of Exceptional Contribution Recognition 2010* for our first book, *How to Haunt Your House*. For all the, **How to Haunt Your House, Book One**, fans who emailed us, left book reviews, or met with us—we want you to know how much we appreciate the encouragement. It gave us the courage to do it once again! We're not a huge home haunt by any means, but we've seen more and more people each year come by and see our little piece of haunt heaven. To all of you—you've made us feel we have reached out in a positive way to keep the Halloween spirit going—*thank you!*

CPSIA information can be obtained
at www.ICGtesting.com
Printed in the USA
LVIC06n2111221013
358091LV00039BA/386